OECD *Economic Surveys*
Electronic Books

The OECD, recognising the strategic role of electronic publishing, will be issuing the OECD *Economic Surveys*, both for the Member countries and for countries of Central and Eastern Europe covered by the Organisation's Centre for Co-operation with Economies in Transition, as electronic books with effect from the 1994/1995 series -- incorporating the text, tables and figures of the printed version. The information will appear on screen in an identical format, including the use of colour in graphs.

The electronic book, which retains the quality and readability of the printed version throughout, will enable readers to take advantage of the new tools that the ACROBAT software (included on the diskette) provides by offering the following benefits:

❑ User-friendly and intuitive interface
❑ Comprehensive index for rapid text retrieval, including a table of contents, as well as a list of numbered tables and figures
❑ Rapid browse and search facilities
❑ Zoom facility for magnifying graphics or for increasing page size for easy readability
❑ Cut and paste capabilities
❑ Printing facility
❑ Reduced volume for easy filing/portability

Working environment: DOS, Windows or Macintosh.

Subscription: FF 1 800   US$317   £200   DM 545

Single issue: FF 130   US$24   £14   DM 40

Complete 1994/1995 series on CD-ROM:

FF 2 000   US$365   £220   DM 600

Please send your order to OECD Electronic Editions or, preferably, to the Centre or bookshop with whom you placed your initial order for this Economic Survey.

OECD
ECONOMIC
SURVEYS

1994-1995

AUSTRALIA

ORGANISATION FOR ECONOMIC CO-OPERATION AND DEVELOPMENT

ORGANISATION FOR ECONOMIC CO-OPERATION AND DEVELOPMENT

Pursuant to Article 1 of the Convention signed in Paris on 14th December 1960, and which came into force on 30th September 1961, the Organisation for Economic Co-operation and Development (OECD) shall promote policies designed:

- to achieve the highest sustainable economic growth and employment and a rising standard of living in Member countries, while maintaining financial stability, and thus to contribute to the development of the world economy;
- to contribute to sound economic expansion in Member as well as non-member countries in the process of economic development; and
- to contribute to the expansion of world trade on a multilateral, non-discriminatory basis in accordance with international obligations.

The original Member countries of the OECD are Austria, Belgium, Canada, Denmark, France, Germany, Greece, Iceland, Ireland, Italy, Luxembourg, the Netherlands, Norway, Portugal, Spain, Sweden, Switzerland, Turkey, the United Kingdom and the United States. The following countries became Members subsequently through accession at the dates indicated hereafter: Japan (28th April 1964), Finland (28th January 1969), Australia (7th June 1971), New Zealand (29th May 1973) and Mexico (18th May 1994). The Commission of the European Communities takes part in the work of the OECD (Article 13 of the OECD Convention).

Publié également en français.

3 2280 00481 3564

Table of contents

Boxes

Tables

Text

Diagrams

Text

BASIC STATISTICS OF AUSTRALIA

THE LAND

Area (1 000 sq. km)	7 682.3	Population of major cities, 1993 (1 000):	
Agricultural area, 1986-87, per cent of total	61	Sydney	3 714
Urban population, 1991, per cent of total	85	Melbourne	3 189
		Brisbane	1 422
		Perth	1 221
		Adelaide	1 071

THE PEOPLE

Population, June 1993 (1 000)	17 662	Civilian employment, 1993 (1 000)	7 680
Number of inhabitants per sq. km	2.3	*of which:* Agriculture	406
Natural increase, 1993 (1 000)	140	Industry[1]	1 823
Net Migration, 1993 (1 000)	44	Other activities	5 451

PARLIAMENT AND GOVERNMENT

Composition of Parliament following latest elections:

Party	Senate	House of Representatives
Australian Democrats	7	–
Australian Labor Party	29	80
Independent	2	2
Greens	2	–
Liberal Party of Australia	30	49
National Party of Australia	6	16
Total	76	147

Present government: Australian Labor Party
Next general elections for House of Representatives: March 1996

PRODUCTION

Gross domestic product, 1993		Gross fixed capital formation, 1993:	
(A$ million)	413 832	Percentage of GDP	19.6

GENERAL GOVERNMENT SECTOR, PER CENT OF GDP, 1993

Current disbursement	36.7	Current revenue	33.7
Current transfers	14.8	*of which:* Direct taxes	16.4

FOREIGN TRADE

Main exports, 1993, per cent of total:		Main imports, 1993, per cent of total:	
Food, beverages and tobacco	15.6	Food, beverages and tobacco	4.4
Raw materials	15.9	Raw materials and fuels	8.3
Fuels	19.7	Chemicals (incl. plastic)	9.5
Metal manufactures	10.0	Metal manufactures	4.6
Machinery and transport equipment	9.2	Machinery and transport equipment	42.1
Other manufactured products	28.9	Other manufactured products	30.8

THE CURRENCY

Monetary unit: Australian dollar	Currency unit per US dollar, average of daily figures:	
	Year 1994	1.3691
	February 1995	1.3429

1. Including mining, electricity, gas and water, and construction.
Note: An international comparison of certain basic statistics is given in an annex table.

This Survey is based on the Secretariat's study prepared for the annual review of Australia by the Economic and Development Review Committee on 2 March 1995.

•

After revisions in the light of discussions during the review, final approval of the Survey for publication was given by the Committee on 29 March 1995.

•

The previous Survey of Australia was issued in April 1994.

Introduction

When the Committee met a little over a year ago to review Australia, the economy was growing at about 3½ per cent, and any marked quickening in the pace of upswing seemed unlikely given modest world economic growth and weak commodity prices. Faced with substantial levels of long term unemployment the government launched a major labour market programme labelled *Working Nation* to help those workers hit hardest by the recent recession. Contrary to earlier expectations, however, economic activity has gained speed briskly in the course of 1994, and unemployment has declined significantly, while inflation has remained low. At the same time, the current external deficit has widened. Chapter I of this *Survey* takes stock of the recent macroeconomic trends and presents projections for the next two years.

With the pace of expansion picking-up, the desire to maintain non-inflationary growth saw monetary policy tighten from mid-1994 on. Macroeconomic policy making is reaching a critical point in terms of avoiding a repeat of earlier boom-and-bust cycles. How much more monetary restraint would be appropriate in light of inflation expectations that may still be entrenched at levels well above the current rate? Should fiscal policy also be tightened further, and if so, by how much? What are the medium-term considerations pertaining to fiscal policy decisions? These are the key issues addressed in Chapter II.

Chapter III is devoted to a discussion of recent progress in structural reform, assessing the measures adopted and identifying what remains to be done. The discussion is focused on major on-going changes in industrial relations, the *Working Nation* labour market programme and a host of initiatives proposed in the Hilmer Committee report to further promote competitive forces in the economy. The special focus of this year's *Survey* is the health-care system; this is discussed in Chapter IV, highlighting its achievements, problems and directions for further reform. Finally, policy conclusions are presented in Chapter V.

I. Recent trends and short-term prospects

Accelerating growth of output and demand

From its trough reached in the June quarter 1991, economic activity picked up only hesitantly during the following four quarters, with real GDP[1] growing by no more than 0.6 per cent in average annual terms. Thereafter, output growth accelerated to 3.1 per cent in fiscal year[2] (FY) 1992/93, about the average of the preceding decade.

From the second half of 1993 onward, economic activity gathered considerable strength, with trend[3] GDP growth rising to 5.5 per cent in the year to the June quarter 1994. The pace of expansion accelerated further in the September quarter 1994, bringing real GDP to a level 6.4 per cent higher than a year earlier and some $12^1/2$ per cent above its trough in the June quarter 1991. Despite the drought in eastern States which sharply reduced farm output and rural incomes,[4] the economy is estimated to have grown on average by a good 5 per cent in 1994, placing Australia among the fastest growing OECD economies in 1994 (growth rates of similar magnitude are estimated only for Denmark, Ireland and New Zealand). The full extent of the acceleration of growth in 1994 did not become evident until the release of the September quarter National Accounts in December which included significant revisions to earlier quarterly data.

Economic growth in 1993 and 1994 was driven by buoyant domestic demand, in particular strong household consumption and private investment, while the real foreign balance contribution to growth was small in 1993 and turned negative in 1994 (Diagram 1). With wages growing only modestly, non-wage incomes falling and employment picking up only in the second half of the year, the subdued growth of real disposable household incomes ($1^3/4$ per cent) left little room for extra consumption expenditure in 1993. However, consumers'

Diagram 1. **CONTRIBUTION TO GDP GROWTH**

As a percentage change of GDP in previous year

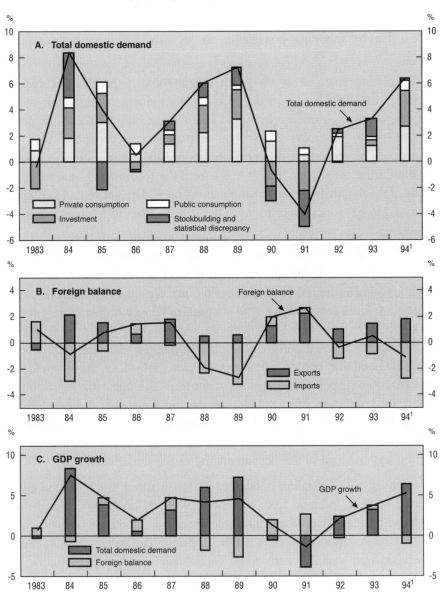

1. OECD estimates.

Source: Australian Bureau of Statistics, *National Accounts.*

3

confidence was on an upward trend from 1990-91 – as shown by the Westpac/ Melbourne Institute Survey – mirroring improved economic and employment prospects. In addition, credit interest rates were at their lowest levels in two decades, thereby inducing households to increase consumption expenditures in 1993.

The picture changed in 1994, when household disposable incomes were boosted by the effect of the strong pick-up in employment on labour incomes, improving incomes from property and entrepreneurship and cuts in personal income taxes in November 1993. Real consumption expenditures rose by an estimated 4½ per cent in 1994, notwithstanding the deterioration in consumer sentiment during the second half of 1994 from the record level attained in June; this was probably attributable to rising interest rates. The household savings ratio is estimated to have increased from 4½ per cent in 1993 to 5½ per cent in 1994.

Dwelling investment has been another mainstay of domestic demand since 1992, after the decline in 1990 and 1991. In the September 1994 quarter its level was 40 per cent higher in real terms than three years earlier. The share of housing investment in GDP rose to about 6¾ per cent in 1994, near the previous peak level of 7 per cent in 1989. The strength in housebuilding largely reflected the extent of pent up demand following the recession and low mortgage interest rates. Moreover, average construction costs remained subdued, partly because sluggish demand for non-dwelling construction helped to avoid supply con-straints in the construction industry. Low housing-loan interest rates in combina-tion with modest house price inflation and rising household disposable income improved the "affordability" of house financing – new loan repayments as a percentage of median family income came down by the middle of 1994 to the low levels experienced in the decade ending in the mid-1980s.[5]

Moreover, the Australian household sector incurred much less debt during the period of asset inflation from the early 1980s through 1989 and, therefore, needed less balance-sheet restructuring compared with both its counterpart else-where and the Australian business sector. Although Australia's personal debt-to-income ratio rose rapidly in response to financial market liberalisation, from some 33 per cent in 1980 to an estimated 50 per cent in 1994, the current level is not high by international standards (for example, latest estimates place the debt-to-income ratios in Denmark, Finland and Sweden between 60 and 100 per cent and those in the United Kingdom and Norway substantially above 100 per cent).

4

However, part of the boom in Australia's residential investment may also be a reflection of inflation expectations guided by past high price and wage inflation rather than by the Reserve Bank's objective (see Chapter II). Affordability of house financing deteriorated during the second half of 1994, reflecting higher borrowing costs and rising house prices; by then, pent up demand had also been run off. The first signs of weakening demand for housing credit are already visible in credit statistics, but this is expected to show up in a slowdown in residential investment demand only in 1995.

In contrast to housing investment, business investment remained stagnant during the first two years of the upswing, notwithstanding the temporary strength of machinery and equipment investment in the second half of 1992. Business profitability improved, labour productivity rose, and debt servicing costs declined. But there was also substantial spare technical capacity and businesses were endeavouring to reduce gearing (*i.e.* leverage). This balance sheet restructuring was a major reason why business investment remained weak for a longer period after the recent recession (Diagram 2) than after the 1982-83 downturn,

Diagram 2. **THE CURRENT EXPANSION COMPARED**

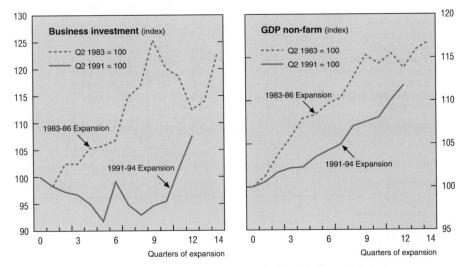

Source: Australian Bureau of Statistics, *National Accounts,* and OECD, *Main Economic Indicators.*

when corporate gearing ratios were lower than in the early 1990s, helping to boost cash flow and interest cover.[6]

However, during 1993 evidence was growing that many companies had significantly improved their balance sheets. Leverage had been reduced, and in

Table 1. **Supply and use of resources**

Percentage changes, 1989/90 prices

	From previous year				From previous period, seasonally adjusted annual rate			
	1993	1994[1]	1992/93	1993/94	1993		1994	1994[3]
	Calendar years		Fiscal years[2]		I	II	I	Q3
Consumption								
Private	2.0	4.5	2.5	2.8	1.4	2.6	4.9	5.6
Public	1.3	4.6	2.2	2.2	2.7	−3.1	12.8	4.9
Gross fixed investment	2.3	13.6	1.7	6.3	0.7	4.7	15.2	17.6
of which:								
Government	0.3	6.7	1.1	−2.5	4.4	−10.9	8.8	14.0
Private								
Total	2.6	14.4	1.8	7.4	0.2	6.9	16.0	18.0
Dwellings[4]	9.6	10.6	9.9	10.9	6.5	14.7	7.9	10.4
Other construction	−4.9	5.1	−8.6	2.5	−1.8	−0.3	12.7	4.6
Equipment	4.7	26.0	6.8	12.5	−2.7	9.6	35.7	29.5
Public enterprises	−10.2	5.6	−13.4	−8.2	−5.4	−10.8	−5.5	23.9
Final domestic demand	1.9	6.4	2.3	3.4	1.5	2.0	8.4	8.0
Change in stockbuilding[5]	0.5	−0.0	0.7	0.1	0.3	0.1	−0.2	0.3
Total domestic demand	2.5	6.3	3.0	3.5	2.0	2.1	7.9	8.3
Exports of goods and services	7.0	8.3	5.7	8.8	5.0	9.8	10.4	8.2
Imports of goods and services	5.1	14.2	7.1	7.3	−0.4	8.9	11.9	18.1
Change in foreign balance[5]	0.5	−0.9	−0.1	0.4	0.5	0.2	0	−1.7
GDP (expenditure-based estimates)	2.9	4.7	2.8	3.9	3.1	2.4	7.7	6.4
Statistical discrepancy[5]	0.8	0.3	0.4	0.3	0.5	0.4	−0.8	−0.1
GDP (income-based)	3.7	5.0	3.3	4.2	4.1	3.3	6.1	6.3
of which:								
Farm	2.8	−2.1	6.3	3.0	0.3	1.6	8.7	−16.4
Non-farm	3.7	5.7	3.1	4.3	4.3	3.4	6.0	7.2
GDP (average measures)[6]	3.4	5.4	3.1	4.2	3.8	2.9	7.1	6.4

1. OECD estimates.
2. Fiscal years begin 1 July.
3. From previous year.
4. Including real estate transfer expenses.
5. As per cent of GDP in the previous period.
6. Average of the expenditure, production and income measures of GDP.
Source: Australian Bureau of Statistics and OECD estimates.

combination with lower nominal interest rates, this improved interest cover and cash flows in the corporate sector.[7] In consequence, plant and equipment investment levels increased over the course of 1993 and trend growth ran at two-digit rates throughout 1994, leading to an average annual increase of about 25 per cent (Table 1). Private non-housing construction as well as investment by government business enterprises also recovered in 1994, raising total business investment by an estimated 16 per cent, the first increase in five years. Hence, the share of business investment in real GDP recovered by $1\frac{1}{4}$ percentage points to $12\frac{1}{2}$ per cent in 1994, still substantially below the 16 per cent high attained in 1989. The low growth of business demand for loans relative to the expansion of nominal investment has been associated with continued strength of equity issues and strongly growing cash flows in 1994. This suggests that for the time being, business financing is relying more on internal sources and new equity than bank loans, and that the recent sharp increase in long-term interest rates is unlikely to affect business investment much in the short run. Such robustness should help to reverse what has been an unfavourable trend in business investment by international standards since the late 1980s, in spite of stronger output growth than elsewhere (Diagram 3).

Public consumption is estimated to have grown quite strongly last year, broadly in line with private consumption, and appears to have been driven by State and local expenditure. A major cause of strong government consumption appears to have been the redundancy payments incurred in the course of restructuring the public sector workforce. There is substantial uncertainty about other reasons for government consumption buoyancy and the possibility of irregular factors playing a role cannot be ruled out. General government investment, which was flat in 1993, recovered markedly in 1994, with the increase estimated to be evenly split between both Commonwealth and State (general government) investment. State (general government) investment has been boosted by the bunching of rail expenditures associated with the "One Nation" statement. With respect to Commonwealth (general government) investment, the increase largely reflects a rise in expenditure by non-budgetary agencies (including the Commonwealth Scientific and Industrial Research Organisation and the Civil Aviation Authority).

Growth in 1994 was broadly based across industrial sectors, with a particularly strong growth in manufacturing – estimated at some 11 per cent in annual

Diagram 3. OUTPUT AND INVESTMENT: AN INTERNATIONAL COMPARISON

Index 1980 S1 = 100

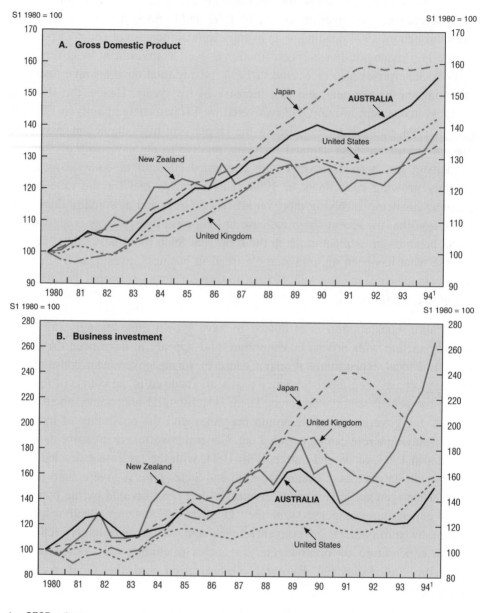

1.   OECD estimates.
Source: OECD.

8

average terms, the highest recorded since the establishment of the statistics in 1974. Even the finance, property and business services sector, which had stagnated in 1993, recovered strongly in the second half of 1994. However, the severe drought in the eastern States entailed a negative contribution to overall growth from the agricultural sector, whose output is estimated to fall by around 20 per cent in FY 1994/95.

The size of the output gap

The strong increase in production over the past two years together with the lagged recovery of business investment led to surging capacity utilisation, particularly in manufacturing. Survey-based indicators suggest that capacity utilisation increased strongly in 1994 to exceed the average of the period since 1980 and more than half of the fall in capacity utilisation in the recession was recouped by mid-1994. This bodes well for the continuation of the investment recovery. On the other hand, the diminishing spare capacity in the economy has a bearing on future inflation and the setting of economic policies. Unfortunately, previous peak levels of capacity utilisation may give an exaggerated impression of *economically viable* spare capacity, given the low rates of investment over recent years. This is in accordance with the notion that the growth of potential output may change significantly over the economic cycle, reflecting *inter alia* the varying growth of the business-sector capital stock. On the other hand, the better use of existing equipment suggested by widespread anecdotal reports may be an influence working in the opposite direction.

Although the capital stock tends to react to *changes* in investment with considerable inertia, the cumulative 25 per cent decline in business investment from 1989 to 1993 was large enough to impart a marked impact on productive potential. According to the OECD's estimates, the growth of the business-sector capital stock fell from 4$\frac{1}{2}$ per cent in 1989 to about 2 per cent in 1992 and 1993, before accelerating to an estimated 2$\frac{1}{2}$ per cent in 1994. The OECD estimates that this contributed to a steady decline in the potential growth of business output from a rate as high as 3$\frac{1}{2}$ per cent in 1988 and 1989 to only 2$\frac{1}{2}$ per cent in 1993, the exact magnitude depending on the assumption about the potential labour force. Business-sector potential output growth is estimated to have recovered to

Diagram 4. **OUTPUT GAPS**
1989-90 prices

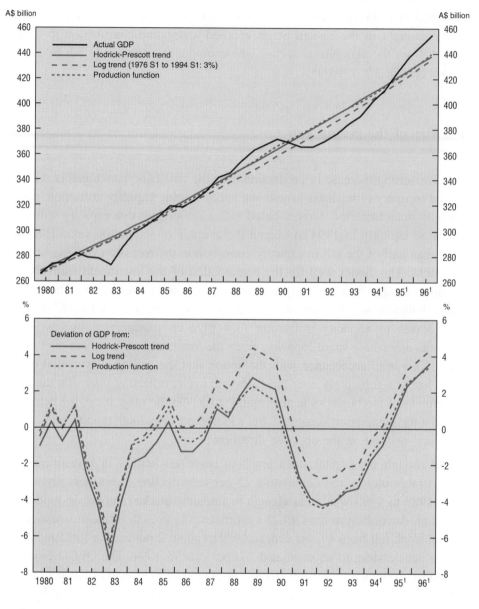

1. S2 1994 to S2 1996 are projections.
Source: OECD.

2³/₄ per cent in 1994 and, on the basis of OECD projections, to be a little above 3 per cent in 1995-96.

There is considerable uncertainty surrounding estimates of potential output and in turn, estimates of the difference between actual output and its estimated potential, the "output gap".[8] Nonetheless, given the strong acceleration of economic growth, all estimates suggest that the output gap has narrowed significantly in 1994. Indeed, the OECD's measure suggests it could have closed by the beginning of 1995 (Diagram 4). On this basis, the OECD's projections presented below, which show economic growth remaining higher than the OECD's estimate of potential growth, imply that inflation pressures are likely to emerge in the course of 1995.

An improving labour market

Unlike the period after the recession of 1982-83 – when total employment rebounded strongly immediately after its decline – employment broadly stagnated in the two years following its fall of 2.4 per cent (seasonally adjusted annual averages, see Table 2) in 1991. As a consequence, fears were voiced that this might be a "jobless recovery". It is, however, regularly observed that in the early stages of an upswing, underutilised technical and human capacity allow expansion of production without any additional factor inputs. This is the more so when the initial recovery in activity is relatively mild, as was the case in 1992. But in 1993 output began to grow more dynamically, and total employment accelerated to a seasonally-adjusted annual rate (s.a.a.r., hereafter) of 4¹/₂ per cent in the December quarter 1993. However, because of sluggish growth in labour demand during the first three quarters and a negative carry-over from the preceding year, annual average employment growth amounted only to ¹/₂ per cent in 1993 (Table 2). With labour demand remaining buoyant thereafter, an average annual employment gain of 3.1 per cent was posted in 1994, with employment reaching its highest recorded level in the December quarter (Diagram 5). This silenced the talk of a "jobless recovery".

Around 275 900 jobs (in trend terms) were created in the course of 1994, of which just over half were full-time jobs. Two-digit employment growth rates were recorded in certain service sectors (cultural and recreational services, communication services, and property and business services). Solid increases (3¹/₂ to

11

Table 2. **The labour market**

Seasonally adjusted

	1991	1992	1993	1994	1994 S1	1994 S2	1994 Nov.	1994 Dec.	1995 Jan.
Civilian labour force[1]	0.5	0.8	0.7	1.8	1.8	1.8	1.4	1.7	1.9
of which:									
Males	0.2	0.6	0.4	1.1	1.1	1.1	1.1	1.2	1.5
Females	1.0	1.2	1.0	2.8	2.8	2.7	1.8	2.5	2.6
Employed persons[1]	-2.4	-0.5	0.6	3.1	2.7	3.6	3.3	3.6	3.6
of which:									
Full-time	-3.7	-2.2	0.8	2.3	1.7	2.9	2.9	2.3	2.6
Part-time	2.8	5.5	-0.2	5.9	5.7	6.0	4.8	7.9	6.9
Unemployment rate[2]	9.6	10.8	10.9	9.8	10.2	9.3	9.3	8.9	9.0
of which:									
Males	6.3	11.4	11.5	10.0	10.6	9.4	9.5	9.0	9.2
Females	9.2	10.0	10.1	9.4	9.7	9.1	9.0	8.8	8.7
Juniors looking for full-time work	27.2	33.0	31.8	30.3	32.7	27.8	27.5	27.0	27.0
Participation rate[2]	63.2	62.9	62.6	63.0	62.8	63.1	63.2	63.2	63.3
of which:									
Males	74.7	74.2	73.7	73.6	73.6	73.6	73.8	73.7	74.0
Females	52.0	52.0	51.8	52.6	52.3	52.9	52.9	53.1	53.0
Overtime (per employee) all industries (hours)[2, 4]	1.1	1.1	1.2	1.3	1.3	1.3	n.a.	1.3	n.a.
Average weekly hours worked[2, 3]	34.4	34.7	34.5	34.7	33.8	35.6	35.7	36.9	26.3
Job vacancies (thousand)[4]	26.2	27.2	34.3	57.4	48.9	66.0	n.a.	66.7	n.a.

1. Per cent change from corresponding period of previous year.
2. Levels.
3. Not seasonally adjusted.
4. Quarterly data based on mid-month of quarter.
Source: Australian Bureau of Statistics, *Labour Force Australia*, Preliminary and Final (catalogue No. 6202.0 and 6203.0); and *Job Vacancies and Overtime* (catalogue No. 6354.0).

4 per cent) were registered in large sectors such as manufacturing, retail trade and construction, accounting together for nearly two-thirds of the newly created jobs. On the other hand, employment fell in government administration and defence – mirroring ongoing efforts to improve efficiency and cut budgetary costs through labour shedding – as well as in mining and in agriculture, forestry and fishing.

The number of part-time jobs grew faster than full-time employment, increasing at a twelve-monthly rate of 6½ per cent in the second half of 1994,

Diagram 5. **OUTPUT AND EMPLOYMENT**

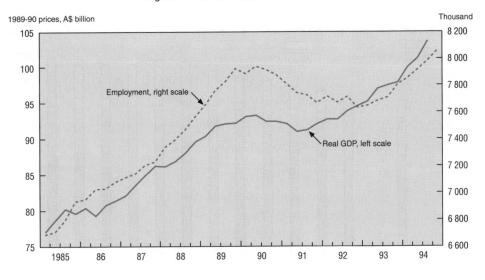

Source: OECD.

compared with 3 per cent for full-time work, which is in accordance with trends observed earlier (Diagram 6). Recent labour force surveys suggest that new entrants into the part-time workforce increasingly prefer part-time to full-time work.[9] Just under half of net growth in part-time work is due to young people aged under 25 years who are frequently still in education and, therefore, unlikely to desire full-time work in addition to full-time study. Another fraction (almost 40 per cent) of part-time employment growth in 1994 were women of prime working age who often have family commitments which prevent full-time working.

The growth of the labour force slowed down from annual rates of 2¹/₂ to 3¹/₂ per cent in 1988-90 to only about 0.6 per cent during the following three years largely as a result of the usual discouraged worker effect during downturns. The growth of the labour force accelerated mildly to 1.8 per cent in 1994, as the result of the growth of the population of working age by some 1.2 per cent and a small increase in the participation rate. As a consequence, the seasonally-adjusted unemployment rate, which had stood stubbornly at around 11 per cent from

13

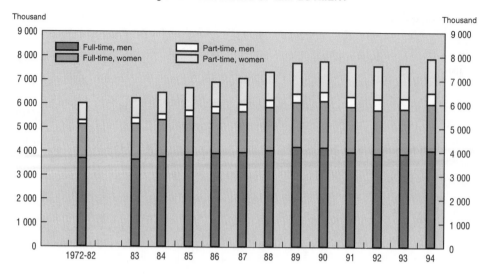

Diagram 6. **PATTERNS OF EMPLOYMENT**

Thousand

Full-time, men   Part-time, men
Full-time, women Part-time, women

1972-82 83 84 85 86 87 88 89 90 91 92 93 94

Source: Australian Bureau of Statistics and OECD.

mid-1992 until the end of 1993, responded vigorously to the pick-up in employ-ment and fell rapidly throughout 1994, to 8.9 per cent in December 1994. In annual average terms, the rate of unemployment decrease by 1.1 percentage points to 9.8 per cent in 1994.

The improvement in the labour market during 1994 also became visible in the rising number of hours worked (up some 4 per cent) and the number of overtime hours worked per week (more than 8 per cent higher). Moreover, the number of job vacancies is likely to have grown by an average of around 70 per cent in 1994. This lowered the unemployment/vacancy (UV) ratio, which is a useful indicator of labour market tightness as it provides a relationship between labour supply and labour demand not realised. The UV ratio had peaked at 36 in mid-1992, *i.e.* on average 36 unemployed competed for every recorded vacancy. It fell gradually to 25 in December 1993, and steeply thereafter to 12 jobseekers per vacancy in December 1994. In the absence of structural change, relatively low rates of vacancies generally co-exist with high rates of unemployment and *vice versa.* Diagram 7 shows that the Australian labour market has moved

14

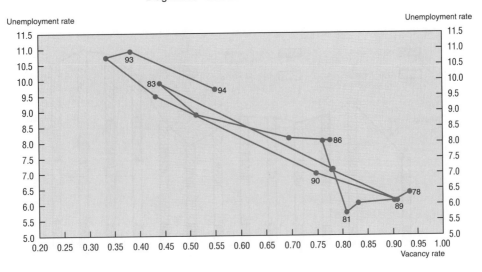

Diagram 7. **THE BEVERIDGE CURVE**[1]

1. Annual vacancy rate based on quarterly data lagged two quarters.
Source: OECD.

downwards on the unemployment-vacancy curve (Beveridge curve) in 1994; there is no evidence as yet for a shift of the curve towards the origin.[10]

The number of people seeking for more than one year for a job has responded quite strongly to the economic recovery, falling on average by 10¼ per cent in 1994 (Diagram 8). As this rate of decrease was steeper than the fall in total unemployment (–8½ per cent), the share of long-term unemployed in total joblessness fell by close to ½ percentage point to some 36 per cent in 1994. These falls in long term unemployment have been broadly consistent with what would normally be expected given the rate of employment growth and the rate of the decline in total unemployment over the last year.

How much further slack is left in the labour market?

Analogous to the issue of the size of the output gap is the question about the remaining cyclical slack in the labour market, which is usually addressed in terms of the non-accelerating inflation rate of unemployment (NAIRU), a proxy for the "natural" rate of unemployment (see also Chapter III). Most Australian studies

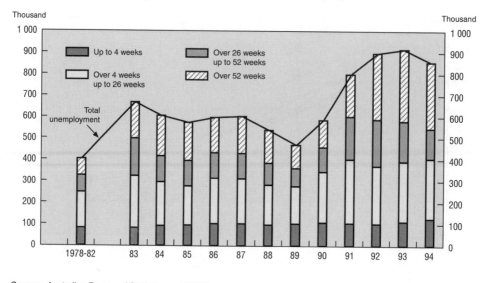

Diagram 8. **STRUCTURE OF UNEMPLOYMENT**

have put the rate at around 7 per cent. However, there is a large degree of uncertainty around these estimates (Table 3). The Beveridge curve, which relates unemployment to unfilled vacancies, indicates that there is no evidence of a significant structural shift in unemployment (see Diagram 7). It is not possible yet to test empirically the degree to which recent reforms, programmes and other factors (including those discussed in Chapter III) may have reduced the "natural" rate of unemployment. In the absence of structural policies to reduce the NAIRU, it is unlikely that a strong cyclical upswing will be sufficient to bring unemployment back below pre-recession levels. The role of structural policies in reducing the NAIRU is discussed in Chapter III.

Low and stable wage and price inflation

As in the post-1983 recovery, the lagged response of labour demand to the current upswing in production meant a marked rise in labour productivity – 2¾ and 3¼ per cent in 1992 and 1993, respectively, followed by an estimated

Table 3. **Indicators of the "natural rate" of unemployment**[1]

Per cent of total labour force

	1970-79	1980-85	1986	1987	1988	1989	1990	1991	1992	1993	1994
NAIRU[2]				6.6	6.3	6.5	6.5	6.6	7.0	7.5	7.4
Beveridge curve indicator[3]	5.4	7.1	7.8	7.7	7.5	7.2	7.1	7.1	7.3	7.6	7.9
Okun curve indicator[4]	3.8	7.7	9.1	9.5	9.9	10.2	10.2	9.8	9.1	8.2	7.2
Hodrick-Prescott filter[5]	5.7	7.0	7.8	8.0	8.2	8.3	8.4	8.5	8.5	8.5	8.5
Actual unemployment rate	3.9	7.6	8.0	8.0	7.0	6.1	7.0	9.5	10.7	10.9	9.7

1. For the methodology of the Beveridge curve and the Okun curve indicators, see Elmeskov (1993).
2. Rolling estimates for the 13 years to the year shown, based on a standard expectations augmented Phillips curve wage equation. See Johnson and Downes (1994).
3. The vacancy data used to construct the Beveridge curve indicator have been adjusted for a break in the series in 1983. Vacancies have also been lagged by two quarters to remove some cyclical dynamics.
4. The capacity utilisation rates used to construct this indicator are lagged two quarters.
5. Low-frequency component of a Hodrick-Prescott filter. See King and Rebello (1989).

Source: OECD.

17

2¼ per cent in 1994. Reflecting the substantial slack in the labour market, average earnings (National Accounts basis) are estimated to have grown only by 1¾ per cent, about the same rate as average "headline inflation" in 1994. The survey-based measure of average weekly earnings suggests slightly faster annual wage growth, 2½ per cent in 1994, higher than the rate registered for 1993 and 1992. Award[11] rates of pay barely grew by a third of that rate in 1994 (Table 4). The "safety net wage increases" under Accord Mark VII[12] for those groups unable to reach agreements – A$ 8 per week not before 1 July 1994 and another A$ 8 per week not before 1 July 1995 – will contribute around 1¼ per cent per year to their earnings over the next two years. This is likely to prevent minimum wages from rising ahead of price inflation.

Wage moderation, combined with labour productivity gains, has reduced the growth in non-farm nominal unit labour costs from rates as high as 6 to 7 per cent in 1988 to 1990, to slightly above 1 per cent in 1992 and broad stability in 1993 and 1994 (Diagram 9). The implicit non-farm GDP deflator rose by around 1 per cent in 1994, in accordance with econometric analysis suggesting that Australia's price inflation is primarily determined by cost factors. As a consequence, real unit labour costs continued their downward trend since late 1991 and are

Table 4. **Costs and prices**

Percentage change from corresponding period of previous year

	1991	1992	1993	1994		
				Q1	Q2	Q3
National Accounts deflators [1]						
Private consumption	3.6	1.7	1.9	1.3	1.5	1.4
Total domestic demand	3.3	1.7	1.8	1.3	1.0	1.2
GDP	2.0	1.5	1.2	0.9	1.4	1.4
Exports of goods and services	−5.0	1.9	1.6	−4.4	−3.3	−5.1
Imports of goods and services	1.2	3.4	4.7	−2.8	−4.1	−6.8
Non-farm GDP	2.6	1.3	1.3	0.9	1.3	0.9
Consumer price index	3.2	1.0	1.8	1.4	1.6	1.9
Average weekly earnings, all employees	3.8	2.5	2.8	2.0	2.8	3.0
Award rates of pay, adults	3.7	2.4	1.0	1.1	1.3	1.2

1. Derived from seasonally adjusted series.
Source: Australian Bureau of Statistics and OECD.

Diagram 9. **LABOUR COST AND PRODUCTIVITY**

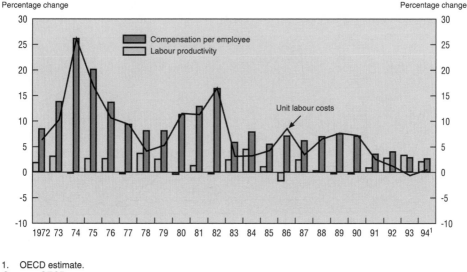

Percentage change

Percentage change

Compensation per employee
Labour productivity

Unit labour costs

1972 73 74 75 76 77 78 79 80 81 82 83 84 85 86 87 88 89 90 91 92 93 94[1]

1. OECD estimate.
Source: OECD.

likely to have fallen by around 1 per cent in 1994, reducing the wage share in national income.

Producer prices also increased quite modestly. Input costs in manufacturing fell from mid-1993 to mid-1994 and have picked up somewhat since then, but in the September quarter 1994, they still were some 2 per cent below their level of a year ago. Manufacturing output prices broadly stagnated during the six quarters to the end of 1994. In the same period, prices of imported goods fell, partly as a result of the effective appreciation of the Australian dollar by more than 10 per cent over this period, but also owing to excess supply and intensified competition in world markets.[13] All this helped to keep the rise in the consumer price index (CPI) to 1.9 per cent in 1994. CPI inflation remained not only below 2 per cent for the third consecutive year, but also lower than the OECD average (excluding Turkey and Mexico) and in line with the average of Australia's five main trading partners (Diagram 10).

But because of the CPI's potential volatility and the fact that some of its components are determined less by markets than by policy decisions, such as

Diagram 10. **INTERNATIONAL COMPARISON OF CONSUMER PRICES**
Change over 12 months

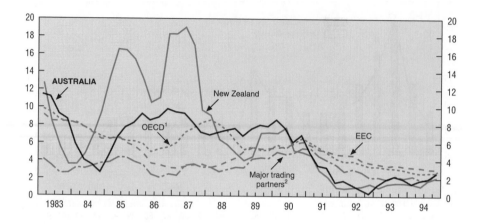

1. Total OECD excluding Turkey and Mexico.
2. Japan, United States, United Kingdom, New Zealand and Korea.
Source: OECD.

changes in tax rates, charges and short-term interest rates, the Reserve Bank of Australia (RBA) focuses on underlying inflation, a concept which adjusts the CPI for these factors (see also the discussion of Monetary Policy in Chapter II). There is, of course, a great variety of potential adjustment methods, which may sometimes lead to markedly different results. However, over the past three years, the difference between various measures of underlying inflation was quantitatively negligible. The authorities have agreed to focus on the Treasury underlying measure[14] as the best-known of the available series. All measures point to underlying inflation of about 2 per cent in 1993 and 1994, without any sign of acceleration in recent quarters.

Although low actual inflation finally led to a break in previously high inflation expectations, they have not yet converged. One indicator, the Westpac/Melbourne Institute Survey, measures consumers' expectations of increases in the CPI in the coming 12 months. This indicator came down from above 10 per cent in the 1980s to around 4½ per cent in late 1993/early 1994 but is still more than double the actual inflation rate. This suggests that it takes considerable time to establish low inflation in people's expectations. It appears that the Westpac/Melbourne measure trended slightly upward in the past three quarters (Diagram 11), which coincides with growing evidence of a rapidly closing output gap.

The difference between the nominal 10 year Treasury bond yield and the real yield on indexed Treasury bonds of about the same maturity can be taken as a proxy of the financial markets' long-term price expectations.[15] This measure stood at $3^{1}/_{4}$ per cent at the beginning of 1994 and rose by nearly $1^{3}/_{4}$ percentage points to about 5 per cent at the end of 1994, corroborating the notion of a rise in inflation expectations. It thus appears that financial market participants are still not fully convinced about the monetary authorities' ability or resolve to maintain low inflation.

Diagram 11. **ACTUAL, UNDERLYING AND EXPECTED INFLATION**

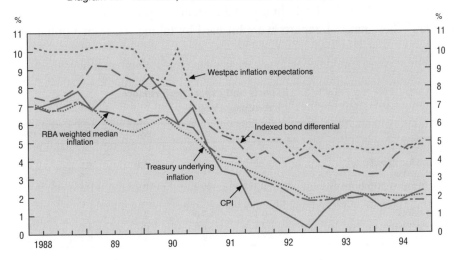

Source: Reserve Bank of Australia, University of Melbourne, Institute of Applied Economic and Social Research, OECD, *Main Economic Indicators.*

Rising external imbalance

Growth of Australia's export markets has accelerated substantially, from 5½ per cent in 1993 to an estimated 11 per cent in 1994, reflecting in particular a pick-up in import demand in Australia's main OECD trading partners, especially Japan. At the same time exporters still benefited from the positive impact of the real effective depreciation of the Australian dollar from 1989 to 1993 on competitiveness (both in terms of relative unit labour costs and relative export prices expressed in a common currency). The recent effective appreciation – by around 10 per cent during 1994 – reversed only part of that competitiveness gain (Diagram 12). This strength of the Australian dollar appears to have forced exporters to make price concessions and to accept lower profit margins (Table 5). These factors underpinned, on balance, a continuation of relatively brisk export growth – with volumes growing at an annual rate of 9½ per cent in the first three quarters of 1994.

Exports of manufactures, growing by close to 20 per cent in volume terms, were the major beneficiary of buoyant Asian markets, now the most important destination for Australian manufactured exports. But due to falling prices of manufactured exports, revenues increased by 13¼ per cent. Farm product exports also performed very well in 1994; the effect of drought on rural exports, adding possibly as much as A$ 1.5 billion to the current external deficit, will only show in 1995.[16] Raw material exports were hit hard by falling Australian dollar prices

Table 5. **Exports and export performance**
Percentage changes

	1990	1991	1992	1993	1994[1]
Volumes					
Merchandise exports	7.2	15.8	5.0	6.1	8.8
Export markets	4.3	5.0	5.7	5.5	10.0
Relative export performance[2]	2.8	10.2	–0.7	0.5	–1.1
Prices					
Export prices	–0.1	–7.0	2.2	1.7	–2.9
Unit labour costs	7.4	2.6	0.7	1.0	–0.6
Profit margins[3]	–7.0	–9.3	1.5	0.7	–2.3

1. Estimates.
2. Differential between export growth and export market growth.
3. Differential between export price growth and unit labour cost growth.
Source: OECD.

Diagram 12. COMPETITIVENESS AND TRADE[1]
Index 1987 = 100

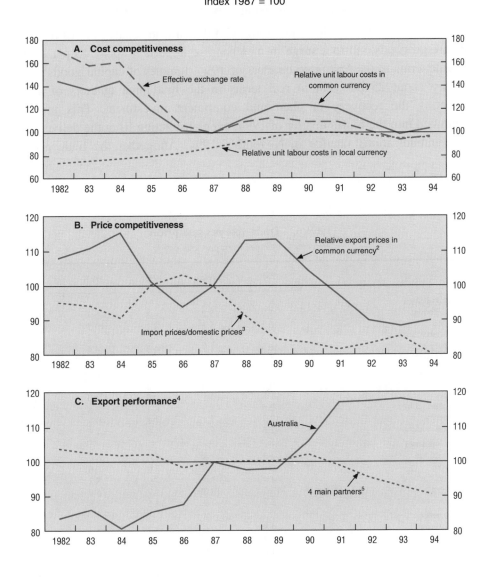

1. 1994 figures are Secretariat estimates.
2. Manufactures.
3. Import prices of total goods and services divided by deflator of total domestic demand.
4. Ratio between export volumes of manufactures and export markets for manufactures.
5. Japan, United States, United Kingdom, and New Zealand.
Source: OECD.

of minerals and energy, so that export revenues fell by 3½ per cent in the first three quarters of 1994 in spite of rising export volumes (Table 6).

Vigorous domestic demand, along with the shift in relative prices in favour of foreign goods, led to a surge in merchandise imports – up by 13 per cent in volume terms in the first three quarters of 1994. Imports of capital goods soared (up by about 25 per cent in real terms in the first three quarters of 1994), reflecting the recovery in plant and equipment investment. This probably continued into the fourth quarter of 1994, even abstracting from the delivery of a telecommunications satellite in November 1994. Altogether the trade account

Table 6. **Trade volumes and prices**

Percentage changes from previous period

	1990	1991	1992	1993	1994 S1 [1]
Export volumes					
Total goods	7.7	15.2	4.8	5.7	11.4
Food	6.1	5.1	2.1	10.3	9.9
Manufactures	14.5	18.9	8.7	8.2	12.7
Energy	16.5	11.7	6.6	4.4	11.5
Raw materials	–5.1	22.3	–0.1	–1.6	8.0
Export prices					
Total goods	–0.1	–7.0	2.2	1.7	–9.3
Food	–1.8	–6.5	9.5	4.0	–4.3
Manufactures	–2.6	–5.5	0.1	3.8	–9.5
Energy	12.7	1.2	1.1	–0.4	–17.0
Raw materials	–2.6	–15.6	–1.0	–4.6	–5.3
Import volumes					
Total goods	–4.8	–1.5	9.0	6.4	10.4
Food	0.6	0.6	3.0	6.6	8.3
Manufactures	–4.4	–3.0	7.9	5.2	10.6
Energy	–17.7	19.0	13.7	16.0	8.8
Raw materials	–3.3	–0.9	14.5	8.8	8.5
Import prices					
Total goods	2.6	0.6	3.2	5.3	–10.5
Food	–0.3	3.1	3.7	4.4	–4.8
Manufactures	1.6	0.6	4.1	6.8	–9.9
Energy	27.0	–10.4	–3.8	2.4	–26.0
Raw materials	0.5	3.8	1.3	0.1	–6.5
Memorandum item:					
Terms of trade					
Total goods	–2.6	–7.5	–1.0	–3.4	1.3

1.   Seasonally-adjusted annual rate over previous half-year.
Source: Australian Bureau of Statistics.

posted a substantial deficit of A$ 4.4 billion in 1994, after a surplus of A$ 2.1 billion in 1992 and a small deficit in 1993 (Table 7).

In recent years, the net services balance improved substantially on account of rapidly expanding tourism exports and business services, bringing the net services deficit down from A$ 2.7 billion in 1992 to A$ 1 billion in 1994. The balance on net factor income and transfers deteriorated somewhat in 1994 after an improvement in 1993, mainly on account of rising "other property income" payments, such as cinema and television royalties, patents, copyrights and licenses. The net unrequited transfers surplus remained at a low level, reflecting lower migrants' transfers than in the early 1990s. Altogether, with few offsetting forces, most of the deterioration of the trade account translated into a worsening current external deficit in 1994, which stood at around A$ 19 billion, about 4½ per cent of GDP, but rose above 5 per cent of GDP in the second half of 1994. The current-account deficit had already widened slightly, from A$ 14.4 billion in 1992 to A$ 15.2 billion in 1993 (some 3¾ per cent of GDP in both years).

Despite the rising current external deficit, net foreign liabilities, which stood at A$ 237.5 billion at the end of 1993, changed little during 1994, thanks to the favourable valuation effect of the appreciation of the exchange rate on the stock

Table 7. **Current account trends**[1]

A$ billion

	1989	1990	1991	1992	1993	1994		
						Q1[2]	Q2[2]	Q3[2]
Exports	46.7	50.3	53.9	57.8	62.2	15.8	16.2	15.9
Imports	51.0	49.9	49.4	55.7	62.4	15.8	16.8	17.8
Trade balance	−4.3	0.5	4.5	2.1	−0.2	−0.1	−0.6	−1.9
Services, net	−20.1	−21.8	−19.5	−18.0	−15.5	−3.6	−4.4	−3.9
Investment income, net	−14.4	−17.0	−15.9	−14.1	−13.0	−2.9	−3.6	−3.3
Non-factor services, net	−5.7	−4.9	−3.6	−3.9	−2.6	−0.7	−0.8	−0.6
Private transfers	2.7	2.5	2.7	2.0	1.1	0.3	0.2	0.3
Official transfers	−0.2	−0.2	−0.3	−0.5	−0.6	−0.2	−0.3	−0.2
Invisibles, net	−17.6	−19.5	−17.1	−16.4	−15.1	−3.5	−4.4	−3.8
Current balance	−22.0	−19.1	−12.6	−14.4	−15.3	−3.6	−5.0	−5.8

1. OECD definitions.
2. Seasonally adjusted.
Source: OECD.

of foreign liabilities. Net external debt fell from A$ 169.7 billion (41 per cent of GDP) at end-1993 to A$ 160.3 billion (some 36 per cent of GDP) at the end of September 1994. This fall largely reflected the financial restructuring of the corporate sector as well as the strong domestic equity market. The stock of foreign debt fell throughout most of 1994, as the corporate sector reduced its debt, while the stock of equity rose by 28½ per cent in the year ending in September 1994, to a historical high of A$ 75 billion. Portfolio investment made up the bulk of the equity inflows, as foreign investors sought to benefit from the high returns available on Australian shares. The net debt servicing ratio – defined as interest paid on net external debt as a percentage of total exports of goods and services – improved from 12.1 per cent in mid-1993 to 11.1 per cent at end-September 1994, well below the peak of 21 per cent recorded in 1990. Strong exports and lower world interest rates helped reduce this ratio, but the recent global rise in interest rates will add to future interest payments on foreign debt.

The outlook to 1996

Current economic indicators and policy assumptions

Current economic indicators point to high growth in late 1994 and early 1995, though not at quite the pace experienced in the first three quarters of 1994. Retail sales and motor vehicle registrations have remained buoyant, merchandise import growth has been strong, business credit demand is recovering and the Westpac coincident index has risen sharply. At the same time, there are no signs of rising price and wage inflation, despite high levels of capacity utilisation in the manufacturing sector and rapidly falling unemployment; high labour productivity growth, which is undoubtedly cyclical in part, and an appreciating Australian dollar have contributed to continuing low rates of inflation.

So as to slow the economy to more sustainable growth rates, monetary policy was tightened in three steps from August 1994 to December 1994, raising the official cash rate by a total of 275 basis points (see Chapter II). In view of the authorities' commitment to maintaining low inflation, it is assumed for the projections presented below that monetary policy is tightened further in the course of 1995 and is unchanged in the following year. Fiscal policy settings are those of mid-January 1995, including the Commonwealth Government's commitment to achieve a budget surplus in FY 1996/97, two years earlier than previously anticipated.

The other main assumptions underlying the projections are that:

- real non-oil commodity prices rise in 1995 and 1996, contributing to a small increase in Australia's terms of trade;
- growth in Australian export markets is projected to be 10 per cent in 1995 and 9 per cent in 1996;
- nominal exchange rates remain unchanged from their levels of 1 March 1995, implying a depreciation of the effective exchange rate of $3\frac{3}{4}$ per cent in 1995 from the second half of 1994;
- the average price of internationally traded oil is US$15.85 per barrel in 1995 and rises in line with OECD manufactured export prices in 1996.

The projections embody information available in mid-March 1995.

Prospects

Output growth is projected to slow from over 5 per cent in 1994 to around 4 per cent in 1995 and $3\frac{1}{2}$ per cent in 1996 (Table 8). This slowing reflects an easing in growth in nearly all the components of demand, including in particular the downturn in the dwelling sector and a decline in the growth in government final demand. In the case of business investment, the growth in 1994 was from depressed levels and, as such, could not be expected to continue indefinitely at such spectacular rates. With the impetus to business investment from the backlog of projects delayed until business confidence and corporate balance sheet positions improved waning and with interest rates higher, a progressive slowing in the growth in business investment is projected. Residential investment has now passed the peak of its cycle and this slowing also should be reinforced by rising interest rates. The declining real growth in government expenditures reflects the government's commitment to lower the budget deficit including by reducing government outlays as a percentage of GDP.

Total employment is projected to continue to grow at around 3 per cent in 1995 but to ease slightly in the following year, to about $2\frac{3}{4}$ per cent; and this slowing contributes to the projected weakening in growth in private consumption in 1996. With rising labour force participation, this employment growth is pro-

Table 8. **Short-term prospects**

Percentage changes

	Percentage share of GDP 1991 current prices	Calendar year			
		1993	1994	1995	1996
A. Demand and output					
at constant 1989/90 prices					
Consumption					
Private	62.1	2.0	4.5	4.2	3.2
Public	18.3	1.3	4.7	4.5	–2.0
Gross fixed investment	20.5	2.3	13.6	6.9	4.5
of which:					
Government	2.4	0.3	6.7	4.2	2.5
Private					
Total	18.1	2.6	14.4	7.2	4.8
Dwellings[1]	5.7	9.6	10.6	–7.0	–7.0
Other construction	3.2	–4.9	5.1	17.0	13.0
Equipment	6.2	4.7	26.0	16.0	10.0
Public enterprises	3.1	–10.2	5.6	11.0	7.0
Final domestic demand	100.8	1.9	6.4	4.9	2.6
Change in stock building[2]	–0.7	0.5	0.1	0.6	0.4
Total domestic demand	100.2	2.5	6.5	5.4	3.0
Exports of goods and services	18.0	7.0	8.5	5.5	10.0
Imports of goods and services	17.4	5.1	15.4	12.0	7.0
Change in foreign balance[2]	0.5	0.5	–1.1	–1.3	0.6
Statistical discrepancy[2]	–0.7	0.8	0.0	–0.1	0.0
GDP(I) at constant prices[3]	100.0	3.7	5.3	4.0	3.6
GDP(A) at constant prices[4]		3.4	5.4	4.0	3.6
B. Other items					
Private consumption deflator		1.9	1.4	2.7	3.7
Employment		0.3	3.1	3.0	2.7
Unemployment rate (per cent)		10.9	9.7	8.6	7.8
General government financial balance[5]		–3.7	–4.7	–3.0	–1.3
Current balance (A$ billion)		–15.3	–20.3	–27.9	–26.9
Current balance[5]		–3.7	–4.6	–5.9	–5.3

1. Including real estate transfer expenses.
2. Contributions to growth.
3. Income measures. Includes statistical discrepancy.
4. Average of the expenditure, production and income measures of GDP.
5. Per cent of GDP.
Source: OECD.

jected to lower the unemployment rate to just under 8 per cent in 1996. Tightening labour-market conditions and the spreading of the "safety net" award wage increases agreed in August 1994 should contribute to rising growth in average earnings over the next two years; even so, earnings growth is expected to remain relatively moderate for this stage of the business cycle. Nevertheless, strong demand growth and some wage acceleration, together with a cyclical slowdown in productivity growth, are projected to underpin a temporary rise in the underlying inflation rate to around 3¾ per cent in 1996.

Import-volume growth is projected to slow in 1995 as the growth in aggregate demand slackens and exogenous imports (such as aircraft) fall. Growth in export volumes is projected to be depressed in 1995 as a result of the drought in the Eastern States but to be boosted in 1996 by a return to normal climatic conditions. Taken together, these trends imply that the external sector will make a negative contribution to growth in 1995 of a similar order to that in 1994 but a positive contribution in 1996. The current account deficit is projected to rise from around 5¼ per cent of GDP in the second half of 1994 to almost 6 per cent of GDP in 1995 but to fall back to 5¼ per cent of GDP in 1996.

Upside risks to the forecasts could include faster than projected growth in the world economy, or the tightening in monetary and fiscal policies not being sufficient to address adequately inflation and current account pressures. If the gap between actual output and trend output did indeed close at the beginning of 1995, as suggested by the OECD's estimates, continuing high growth would contribute to a build-up in inflationary pressures. Wage increases could be higher than projected, particularly in view of the spread of enterprise bargaining and the recent claims for large wage increases made by some major unions. On the other hand, wage increases should pose less of a risk to inflation than in the past insofar as they apply in a decentralised way and are now more likely to be backed by productivity growth.

II.   Economic policy

The challenge to economic policy

The strengthening in economic activity since mid-1993 owes much to the supportive stance of monetary and fiscal policy followed since 1991. At the same time, the 1990/91 recession resulted in substantial slack capacity and raised unemployment to unprecedented levels, bringing price and wage inflation down to low rates. With capacity utilisation rising quickly, the labour market improving rapidly, and the current external deficit widening, macroeconomic policy is being tightened in order to slow the pace of economic expansion to a more sustainable rate so as not to jeopardise continued low inflation. The challenge to economic policy is to avoid the "boom-and-bust" cycles experienced in the past, while pursuing further microeconomic reform in order to improve efficiency and to increase the sustainable rate of growth.

Monetary policy

Objectives and indicators of monetary policy

Since the late 1980s, monetary policy has been oriented towards keeping inflation low, based on increasing recognition that in the long run this course is consistent with the pursuit of the multiple objectives prescribed in the Reserve Bank Act of 1959. In recent years, the Reserve Bank of Australia (RBA) made explicit that a reasonable degree of price stability can be considered to be achieved when the *underlying* rate of inflation stays on average at around 2 to 3 per cent over the course of the economic cycle;[17] and in its *1994 Report and Financial Statements* (p. 3), the RBA reiterated its commitment to this target. The focus is on the underlying rate of inflation which adjusts the overall change in the

CPI ("headline" inflation) for identifiable extraneous factors. In particular, it eliminates the effect of mortgage interest-rate changes on the home ownership component of the consumer price index. Deviations of underlying inflation from the target range may be tolerated as long as they are regarded as temporary.

By its policy approach, the RBA seeks to provide evidence of its commitment to price stability without being bound to any single operational rule. Although the RBA's strategy is somewhat different from the inflation targeting as pursued by New Zealand (since 1990), Canada (since 1991), the United Kingdom (since 1992), and Sweden and Finland (since 1993), *de facto* it comes very close to it. In theory, inflation targeting is thought to be most likely to succeed when it is based on an explicit statement of price stability as the *sole* objective of monetary policy and an institutional framework which makes the Central Bank accountable for inflation outcomes. But whether the existence of all or some of these conditions will lead to inflation outcomes elsewhere permanently superior to those of Australia – as some would predict – remains to be seen. So far, the approach adopted by the RBA has allowed it to achieve a remarkable degree of price stability, in line with inflation performance of countries pursuing explicit inflation targeting.

Monetary conditions are assessed and monetary policy is conducted by the RBA with reference to a set of indicators of future trends in inflation and economic activity. These indicators include the degree of slack in the economy (the "output gap"), changes in expected inflation, wage developments, the price setting behaviour of firms, the terms of trade, nominal and real interest rates, money and credit aggregates, the stance of fiscal policy and the exchange rate. No explicit weighting is attached to these indicators, so that the "art of monetary policy" (Fraser, 1994) is to make an assessment on how any of these variables may be foreshadowing future inflation and activity. In particular, the RBA still feels that as yet none of the monetary aggregates has re-established a sufficiently stable relationship to key macroeconomic variables to permit them to be used as intermediate monetary targets.[18] However, broader monetary aggregates are likely to have been less affected by financial innovation than narrow concepts and could therefore provide some useful information on demand conditions.

Recent financial market developments and the setting of monetary policy

The setting of monetary policy has been complicated by the uncertainty about the underlying strength of economic activity which prevailed from the middle of 1993 to mid-1994. The cuts effected from January 1990 to March 1993 had brought the cash rate – the key policy interest rate – down from above 18 per cent at the end of 1989 to 5¼ per cent in March 1993. The extraordinary magnitude of this cumulative decrease in part bears witness to the transition of the economy from a high inflation environment to a broadly stable price level (Diagram 13). It is, however, also indicative of a high degree of monetary stimulus given to the economy by the middle of 1993. At that time, the recovery was underway but, with continued slack in the economy and a benign outlook for inflation, policy makers remained concerned about stagnant employment, stubbornly high unemployment and weak business investment so that in July 1993, the cash rate was lowered for the fifteenth time in a row, by ½ percentage point to 4¾ per cent.

Diagram 13. **THE CHANGED INFLATION ENVIRONMENT**
Consumption deflator, annual per cent change

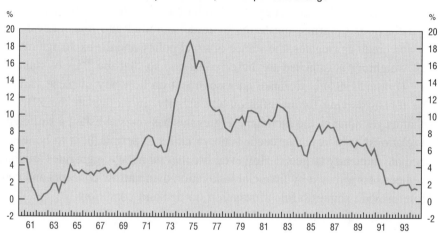

Source: OECD.

In September 1993, hence only two months after the last cash rate cut, employment – typically a lagging indicator of activity – began to pick up strongly. But without evidence of activity itself accelerating and with indications of still substantial excess capacity in 1993 and into 1994 and no signs of increased price or wage inflation pressures, the RBA left the cash rate at its low level for about one year.

A marked change in monetary conditions occurred at the beginning of February 1994, when interest rates in world capital markets picked up in response to a tightening of monetary policy in the United States. In Australia, the long-term government bond[19] rate rose from its trough of 6.4 per cent in January 1994, the lowest level for twenty years, to about 9½ per cent by mid-1994 (Diagram 14, Panel A). This not only exceeded the response of US long-term interest rates to monetary tightening, but was also substantially more than in most other OECD countries (Diagram 15). With short-term interest rates steady from July 1993 until mid-1994, the rise in bond rates implied a marked steepening of the (positive) slope of the yield curve (Diagram 14, Panel B). This coincided with mounting evidence of the recovery taking hold and the related concerns of financial market participants about the inflation outlook as well as widespread expectations that the RBA would have to raise short-term interest rates.

During the first half of 1994, the actual rate of economic expansion exceeded any estimate of potential output growth by a substantial margin. Although there was little doubt that the *level* of aggregate output was still below potential and the actual unemployment rate considerably above NAIRU esti-mates, the speed of the narrowing of the output gap ran the risk of becoming excessive, thereby threatening to kindle inflationary pressures even in the pres-ence of a still positive "output gap" (*via* so-called "speed limit" problem). In addition, in view of the well-known lagged response of economic activity to changed monetary parameters,[20] the prevailing supportive stance of monetary policy became increasingly inappropriate. The RBA thus announced[21] a change in the course of monetary policy, raising the cash rate from 4¾ per cent to 5½ per cent in August 1994.[22] The move came just a day after a half-point rise in the United States' Federal funds and discount rates and was the first increase in the cash rate in five years.

With an increasing number of indicators pointing to further acceleration of the economic expansion, notwithstanding the losses in agricultural output due to

Diagram 14. INTEREST AND EXCHANGE RATES[1]

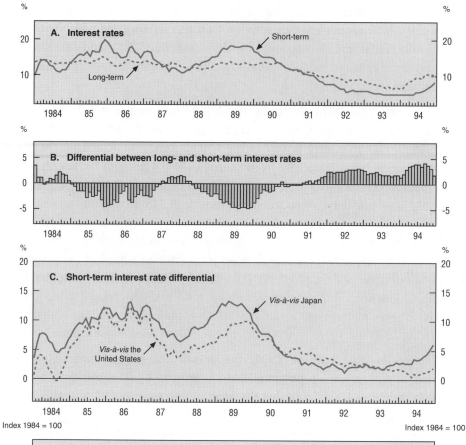

%

A. Interest rates

20   Short-term

10   Long-term

1984   85   86   87   88   89   90   91   92   93   94

%

B. Differential between long- and short-term interest rates

5

0

-5

1984   85   86   87   88   89   90   91   92   93   94

%

C. Short-term interest rate differential

20

15

10   Vis-à-vis Japan

5   Vis-à-vis the
         United States

0

1984   85   86   87   88   89   90   91   92   93   94

Index 1984 = 100

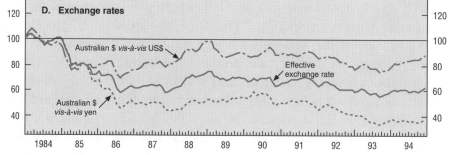

D. Exchange rates

120

100   Australian $ vis-à-vis US$

80   Effective
                                                      exchange rate
60

        Australian $
40   vis-à-vis yen

1984   85   86   87   88   89   90   91   92   93   94

1.   All interest rates are nominal rates.
Source: OECD, *Main Economic Indicators.*

34

Diagram 15. **INTERNATIONAL COMPARISON OF LONG-TERM INTEREST RATES**
Ten-year bond yields

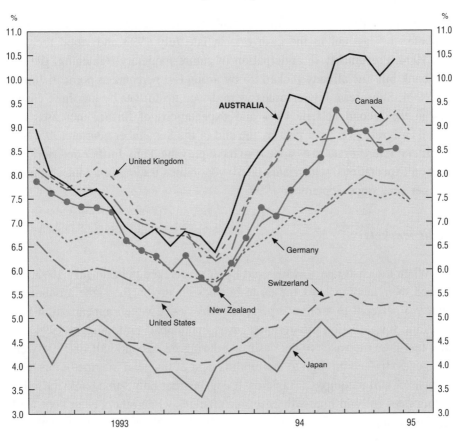

Source: OECD.

the drought, the RBA raised the cash rate again by 1 percentage point to 6½ per cent in October 1994. This hike was both greater and came sooner than financial market participants generally had anticipated. It thus underlined the RBA's determination to lock in low inflation. In December 1994, when third-quarter National Accounts data indicated twelve-monthly economic growth of 6½ per cent, the RBA raised the cash rate by another 1 percentage point, driving it up to 7½ per cent.[23]

The interest rate on three-month bank bills had come down to about 4.8 per cent after the last cut in the cash rate in late July 1993 and stood there until May 1994. Presumably in anticipation of future monetary tightening, the short-term bank bill rate already picked up by around ½ percentage point in June and July 1994. Short-term interest rates were driven up further by the three cash rate rises in the second half of 1994 and expectations of further increases in the official cash rate to 8.5 per cent by the end of the September quarter 1995. So far, the official interest rate rises appear to have prevented any further deterioration in inflation expectations, with yields on 10 year bonds trading in a range from 10 to 10¾ per cent since September 1994.

Credit markets

When the cash rate was lowered by ½ percentage point in July 1993, banks reduced their lending rates for large business loans by the same amount, from about 9½ per cent to around 9 per cent. This level, which appears high for the prevailing low-inflation environment, was maintained until August 1994. Naturally, the three increases in the cash rate during the second half of 1994 were to be expected to feed through to the funding cost of financial intermediaries. But on the basis of still incomplete statistics, it appears that only some banks raised their lending rates fully in line with cash rate changes while others even kept lending rates constant until the December quarter of 1994. This may be interpreted as sign of enhanced price competition among banks.

So far, the relatively high level of lending rates has not prevented a strong recovery of total private-sector credit demand from its recession-induced low level. Starting from the trough[24] reached during the first half of 1992, total credit extended to the private sector began to pick up and attained seasonally-adjusted annualised growth rates between 10 and 12 per cent from May 1994. A break-down of total credit data shows that, so far, credit growth has been driven primarily by credit for housing, while credit demand by business fell during the three years ending in early 1994 and recovered only modestly through the remainder of 1994, to seasonally-adjusted annual rates of around 3 per cent by late 1994 (Table 9). Personal credit demand was also on a downward trend for

Table 9. **Major financial aggregates**[1]

Quarterly, seasonally adjusted

	June 1991	Dec. 1991	June 1992	Dec. 1992	March 1993	June 1993	Sept. 1993	Dec. 1993	March 1994	June 1994	Sept. 1994	Dec. 1994
Credit by financial intermediaries												
	Percentage change from previous period, at annual rates											
Total	-1.6	-2.1	0.0	-1.7	5.3	4.2	4.5	7.2	7.0	10.6	10.9	10.5
Housing	7.4	13.1	14.9	16.7	17.8	19.4	21.4	22.1	22.4	25.0	23.6	16.9
Personal	-2.2	-5.8	-2.7	1.5	-2.3	-0.9	0.5	3.3	1.4	9.5	6.9	10.1
Business	-7.7	-6.9	-5.3	-10.3	0.8	-2.4	-3.5	-0.4	-1.0	1.8	3.3	6.0
	Percentage change from corresponding period of previous year											
Currency	13.9	7.0	4.0	6.8	6.4	6.9	6.3	5.8	7.0	6.7	6.5	6.1
M1	6.9	7.3	14.5	13.3	15.3	16.8	12.7	19.0	19.5	17.4	15.5	9.9
M3	5.2	1.4	2.4	4.2	6.7	6.4	5.8	6.1	6.7	6.7	7.7	9.3
Broad money	1.7	-0.3	1.4	2.0	4.1	4.1	3.4	4.3	5.7	6.3	7.9	9.7

1. Monetary aggregates have been adjusted by the RBA for breaks in the series. These include, for example, changes in the number of corporations reporting, changes in reporting procedures and a transfer of loans from the private sector to the government sector.
Source: Reserve Bank of Australia.

about three years, but turned around in late 1993 and reached annualised growth rates of about 9 per cent by mid-1994.

A surge in housing loans – which recorded annualised three-monthly percentage changes in the range of 20 to 26 per cent from February to September 1994 after strong growth during 1993 (about 20 per cent) and during 1992 (around 15 per cent) – was a matter of concern, with the potential for overheating and, subsequent, abrupt correction. It also appears that the vigorous borrowing for housing at credit interest rates of 8¾ per cent during most of 1994 (and 9½ per cent towards year-end) could have been based on expected inflation much higher than CPI inflation of around 2 per cent. Given the RBA's determination to keep underlying inflation to an average of around 2 to 3 per cent over the business cycle, growth in nominal wages should on average exceed this rate only by the rate of productivity growth.[25] This could render the servicing of housing loans more onerous than many borrowers may have been expecting initially. Moreover, so far, business investment in plant and equipment has been financed largely from internal sources and equity issues. But once the financing of ongoing buoyant business investment requires additional credit from financial intermediaries, household borrowing would need to give way if total credit expansion is to be kept within reasonable limits.

Strong demand for housing loans as the result of low nominal interest rates occurred at the same time that banks were keen to lend for housing due to high interest margins and relatively low risk. Competition amongst the banks was aggressive but was largely focused on interest rates charged to new borrowers. In late 1994, with the entry of new providers of housing finance, margins narrowed somewhat. The rapid growth of housing credit and banks' competition for market share raised the RBA's concern that prudential standards could be undermined. The Reserve Bank thus decided to restrict the 50 per cent risk weight for housing loans to credits for which the loan to valuation ratio is no more than 80 per cent, as from September 1994. For other loans a 100 per cent risk weight will apply.

Other monetary indicators

Strengthening growth of credit to the private sector by financial intermediaries in turn required increased borrowing by the latter, which is reflected in growth of broad monetary aggregates (M3 and "broad money")[26] roughly in line with total credit (Diagram 16). M1, which consists of currency in

Diagram 16. **MONEY AND CREDIT GROWTH**

Percentage change over twelve months earlier

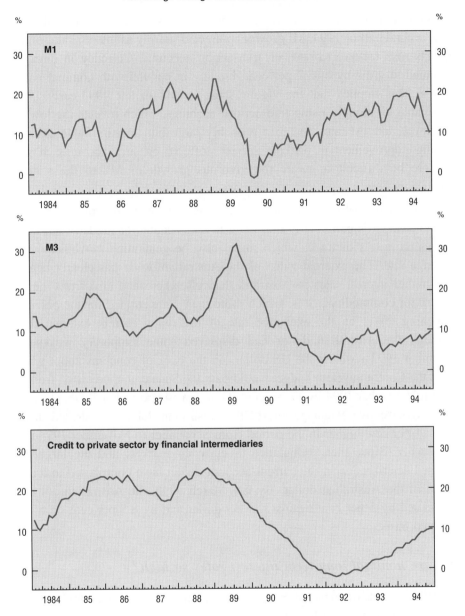

Source: Reserve Bank of Australia and OECD, *Main Economic Indicators.*

circulation and transactions accounts of banks, already grew strongly in 1993, by 15.2 per cent on average. Its growth rate quickened in the first half of 1994, expanding at twelve-monthly growth rates varying between 16 and 20 per cent. In the second half of 1994, MI growth contracted sharply as interest rates on fixed deposits rose relative to rates on transaction accounts. Currency in circulation continued to grow by 6 to 7 per cent, broadly in parallel with nominal national income. This implies that the vigorous rise in M1 in late 1993-early 1994 is attributable to strongly rising transactions accounts, which reflects the low level of nominal interest rates and to a probably large but unquantifiable extent the ongoing improvement in banking services offered on such accounts. It would therefore be difficult to relate the vigorous growth of M1 to the stance of monetary policy.

Another indicator of monetary conditions is the exchange rate. In assessing this indicator, it is particularly important to take account of fundamental factors, such as the terms of trade, which might also be generating movements in the exchange rate. The external value of the Australian dollar has clearly benefited from higher interest rates in Australia than elsewhere and also from the good outlook for commodity prices, which more than compensated for the potentially weakening effect on the exchange rate of the rising current external deficit. Although the Australian dollar had displayed some temporary weakness in September 1993 *vis-à-vis* the US dollar, on the back of concerns about whether or not the Commonwealth budget would pass the Senate, it appreciated from then on until November 1994 by 17 per cent (Diagram 14 above, Panel D). The (trade-weighted) effective exchange rate of the Australian dollar also drifted upward, being 11 per cent higher in the period from September to November 1994 than a year earlier. Since then, turbulance in currency markets and the larger-than-expected deterioration in the current-account deficit have contributed to a depreciation of the Australian dollar. By late March 1995, the Australian dollar had depreciated by 5 per cent against the US dollar and by 8.5 per cent on a trade-weighted basis.

Why are nominal long-term interest rates so high?

With the rate of consumer price inflation remaining flat (at about 2 per cent), the sharp rise in nominal long-term interest rates by some 4 percentage points in the course of 1994 implies an increase in (conventionally measured) *ex post* real long-term interest rates by the same magnitude. At a level of around 8¼ per cent in late 1994, the *ex post* real bond rate was about 2 percentage points higher than the average of 6.3 per cent over the preceding decade, but still somewhat lower than the real rate recorded in late 1992. Moreover, the current high real bond rate exceeds its mean value of the past ten years by only little more than one standard deviation (which was 1.8 per cent), keeping it well within the range experienced in the past. Several other OECD countries also saw both substantial rises in real bond rates during 1994 as well as high levels by year-end, but most of these countries recorded higher price inflation than Australia (Finland and Sweden being exceptions). Hence, the question arises why Australian capital markets responded so vigorously to the global upward trend of bond yields and the growing strength of the economic recovery.

One plausible hypothesis is that the rise in nominal market interest rates was caused by growing inflation fears, notwithstanding the low actual rate of inflation. Inflation worries may have been kindled by the extraordinary acceleration of economic growth and lingering doubts about the authorities' determination to keep trend inflation within the 2 to 3 per cent target range as the economy strengthens further over the next few years. Such an interpretation of recent long-term interest rate developments is in accordance with the indicator of financial market participants' inflation expectations derived from the yield differential between indexed and non-indexed bonds (see Chapter I). When using Australian index-linked bond yields as an indicator for long-term real interest rates, their rise by about 2¼ percentage points during 1994 comes relatively close to the increase in (*ex post*) real bond rates in the United States.[27]

On the other hand, the Westpac/Melbourne Institute Survey (median)[28] measure suggests only a minor worsening of inflation fears by consumers. But this indicator started to rise from an already high level of expected inflation, which was some 2½ points above actual CPI-inflation. Therefore, using this measure of expected inflation yields a substantially lower *level* of *ex ante* real rates than conventionally measured *ex post* real interest rates. However, the *increase* in the survey-based real bond rates is broadly in line with the movement of the *ex post* real long-term interest rate (Diagram 17). Whatever methods are employed to break up nominal bond rates into inflation expectations and a real yield component, it is clear that both factors contributed to rising nominal long-term interest rates in Australia during 1994.

Diagram 17. **_EX-POST_ AND _EX-ANTE_ REAL LONG-TERM INTEREST RATES**
Ten year maturity

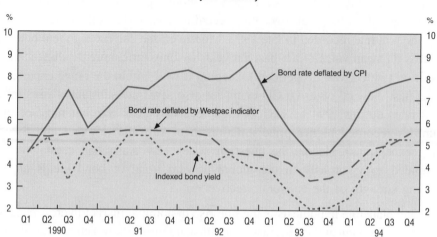

Source: Reserve Bank of Australia, University of Melbourne, Institute of Applied Economic and Social Research, OECD, *Main Economic Indicators.*

The question remains why the real component of the (representative) nominal bond rate has risen substantially since early 1994. To address this question, a variety of potential determinants of real interest rates[29] in OECD countries have been subjected to econometric tests[30] by the OECD. The – still preliminary – estimation results suggest statistically significant upward pressures on Australian real long-term interest rates from higher United States real bond rates, a widening current external deficit, growing uncertainty about the future value of domestic financial assets[31] and increasing real returns on capital (an opportunity cost of holding bonds). The model results are in accordance with the hypothesis of a risk premium demanded by investors in proportion to a long-term average of past inflation relative to expected inflation, which proxies monetary policy credibility by the past record of inflation control.[32] This interpretation of the data is in line with the notion that past poor records of controlling inflation make gaining inflation credibility a slow process.[33]

Fiscal policy[34]

Historical overview

Fiscal policy has supported the recovery in recent years, with the underlying general government budget balance declining by almost 7 percentage points of GDP since the late 1980s to a peak deficit of 5.5 per cent of GDP in FY 1992/93[35] (Diagram 18). Most of this budgetary deterioration was in the Commonwealth budget, which is more sensitive than State budgets to the economic cycle. The Commonwealth budget balance reached a peak of almost 5 per cent of GDP in FY 1992/93, well above previous cyclical highs.[36] Although small in relation to the Commonwealth budget deficit, State[37] government budget deficits also deteriorated sharply in the late 1980s and early 1990s. State government budget

Diagram 18. **GENERAL GOVERNMENT BALANCE**[1]
Fiscal years starting July

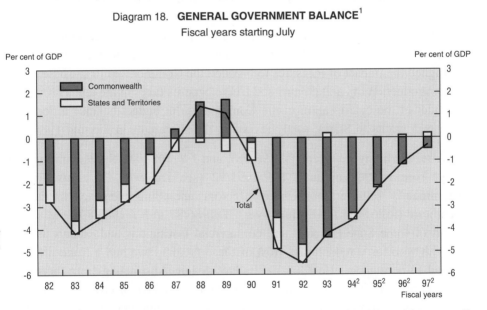

1. This excludes proceeds of extraordinary asset sales and is adjusted to remove the effects of Commonwealth borrowing on behalf of, and lending to, the States and Territories.
2. The projections are based on assumed growth rates which lie midway between those (high and low) shown in the 1995 *National Fiscal Outlook*. Policy settings are those of mid-January 1995. They do not take account of policy intentions which have not been translated into specific policy measures.
Source: National Fiscal Outlook, 1995.

deficits rose from 0.3 per cent of GDP in FY 1988/89 to as high as 1.5 per cent of GDP in FY 1991/92, due in part to a cyclical downturn in revenue growth and the cost of providing financial support to State-backed or State-supported financial institutions.

The deterioration in the Commonwealth budget balance mainly reflects both higher own-purpose outlays and lower revenues, each of which made a similar contribution to the deterioration (Diagram 19). The increase in own-purpose outlays is attributable to both the operation of "automatic stabilisers" during the recession and stimulatory fiscal measures, including labour market programmes and infrastructure spending. Two-thirds of the increase in outlays reflects increased social security expenditure, of which approximately one half is unemployment payments.[38] By contrast, the decline in revenue, which actually started in FY 1987/88, is largely structural. It reflects discretionary reductions in tax revenue in the late 1980s (mainly personal and company tax cuts) and, since then, a decline in indirect tax collections. The main structural factors reducing Commonwealth indirect taxes are lower import tariffs and the fact that the principal indirect tax, the wholesale tax, is not levied on the increasingly large service sector. The structural factors reducing the revenue to GDP ratio have outweighed the impact of measures to broaden the Commonwealth tax base, such as the introduction of capital gains and fringe benefits taxes in the late 1980s. The remainder of the deterioration in the Commonwealth budget balance reflects an increase in grants to States, partly reversing the sharp cuts in the mid-1980s.

After declining between FY 1986/87 and FY 1988/89, State own-purpose outlays rose sharply up until FY 1991/92 (see Diagram 19). This growth predominantly reflected non-cyclical factors, including increases in capital expenditure (following the decline over FY 1986/87 to FY 1988/89), outlays in support of some State financial and commercial institutions and outlays associated with workforce reductions. Most of these factors have had a "one-off", as opposed to permanent effect, on the budget deficit. Abstracting from them, the main contributions to the decline in outlays as a percentage of GDP over the past two years come from falling debt service costs and capital outlays. State revenue recovered as a proportion of GDP between FY 1989/90 and FY 1992/93, in part reflecting an increase in Commonwealth special purpose payments (which was partly related to the anti-recession spending initiatives contained in the "One Nation" policy programme of the Commonwealth government) and structural

Diagram 19. GENERAL GOVERNMENT OUTLAYS AND REVENUE[1]

Fiscal years starting July

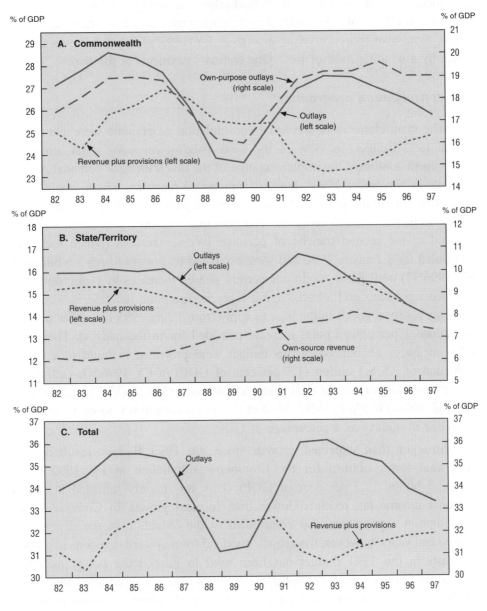

1. See footnotes to Diagram 18.
Source: National Fiscal Outlook, 1995.

45

increases in some State taxes (introduced as part of fiscal consolidation pro-grammes, in various States). The cyclical impact of strong economic growth and the full year effects of the structural increases in some State taxes resulted in very strong State own-source revenue growth in FY 1993/94,[39] but this was largely offset by a winding back of the "One Nation" payments to the States.

The consolidation programme[40]

The main elements of the fiscal consolidation programme were announced in the 1993 Budget. In view of the weak pace of recovery at the time, the government confirmed the implementation of the first tranche of personal income tax cuts in November 1993[41] but also announced measures which would come into effect in future years and result in progressive reductions in the budget deficit from FY 1994/95 onwards. The principal measures announced were the deferral of the second tranche of personal income tax cuts (which had been scheduled for 1 January 1996 and were estimated to amount to A$ 3.6 billion in FY 1996/97) until fiscal conditions permit, phased increases in excise duties on petroleum products and tobacco and a 1 percentage point increase in wholesale sales tax for most goods in the base to apply from 1 July 1995 (in addition to the immediate 1 percentage point increase provided for in the budget). These and other measures announced in this budget were projected to build to a deficit reduction of A$ 8.5 billion (1.7 per cent of GDP) in FY 1996/97, cutting the deficit from 4.0 per cent of GDP (A$ 16.9 billion) in FY 1993/94 to 1.2 per cent (A$ 5.8 billion) in FY 1996/97. Most of this improvement was to be achieved by a decline in outlays as a percentage of GDP.

Stronger than expected growth since the 1993 Budget resulted in a somewhat lower outturn for the Commonwealth deficit in FY 1993/94, at A$ 13.7 billion (3.2 per cent of GDP). This was mainly reflected in higher personal income tax receipts; lower than forecast growth in Commonwealth consumption expenditure also contributed to the reduction in the deficit. For subsequent years, however, the growth dividend from upward revisions in growth forecasts in the 1994 Budget has been used to finance the policy measures announced between the 1993 and 1994 Budgets (Table 10); policies announced in the 1994 Budget had little effect on the deficit. These measures increased estimated outlays by A$ 1.7 billion (0.4 per cent of GDP) in FY 1994/95, rising to A$ 2.1 billion (0.4 per cent of GDP) in FY 1996/97 but had virtually no effect

Table 10. **Effects of policy decisions between the 1993 and 1994 Budgets**

A$ million

	1994/95	1995/96	1996/97
Revenue	−143	−77	−47
Outlays	1 737	2 173	2 118
of which: "Working Nation"	1 067	1 734	1 906
Balance	1 594	2 096	2 071
Memorandum item:			
Revisions to economic parameters			
Outlays	−1 647	−2 155	−2 654

Source: Budget Statements 1994/95.

on estimated revenues. The main policy measures increasing outlays were those contained in *Working Nation,* the programme of active labour market and related policies announced in May 1994 (see Chapter III). The FY 1994/95 Budget deficit is now expected to be 2.6 per cent of GDP (A$ 12.3 billion), instead of 2.5 per cent of GDP (A$ 11.7 billion) as forecast at the time of the FY 1994/95 Budget. However, this increase reflects a delay in the receipt of proceeds from the privatisation of the government airline, Qantas. Abstracting from this, the deficit will be lower than projected at Budget time, with revenue expected to be A$ 2.2 billion – nearly half a percentage point of GDP – higher than forecast due to higher than expected economic growth.

The Government has recently announced that it intends to institute a significant structural tightening of policy in the FY 1995/96 Budget in May. It now intends to bring the Commonwealth budget into surplus by FY 1996/97, two years earlier than previously envisaged. This would represent an improvement of at least 1 per cent of GDP over the consolidation programme planned at the time of the FY 1994/95 Budget.

The medium-term fiscal outlook[42]

The underlying general government budget deficit is estimated to fall to 3.6 per cent of GDP in FY 1994/95. Based on policy settings in mid-January, but abstracting from policy intentions not yet translated into specific policy measures, the underlying general government deficit is projected to fall to 1.1 per cent of GDP in FY 1996/97 and 0.3 per cent pf GDP in the following year (see Diagram 18). The recently foreshadowed acceleration in the Commonwealth fiscal consolidation programme can be expected to reduce further projected budget deficits. The projected reductions in the deficit are mainly attributable to a decline in outlays relative to GDP; the ratio of revenue to GDP is projected to remain relatively flat (see Diagram 19).

The Commonwealth (underlying general government) deficit is estimated to be 3.3 per cent of GDP in FY 1994/95. It is projected to fall to 1.1 per cent of GDP in FY 1996/97 and to 0.5 per cent of GDP in FY 1997/98; allowing for the foreshadowed acceleration in the fiscal consolidation programme would reduce further the projected deficits. The projected reduction in the deficit is mainly attributable to a decline in outlays as a percentage of GDP. Own-purpose outlays are projected to fall back by the end of the outlook period to their level (as a percentage of GDP) of the trough of the recession, but to remain significantly higher than during the late 1980s. This decline mainly reflects cyclical factors, particularly the lower expenditure on social security and welfare resulting from the expected fall in unemployment. Commonwealth revenue (as a per cent of GDP) is projected to grow little and hence will remain lower as a percentage of GDP than in the second half of the 1980s. Despite the phased indirect tax increases announced in the 1993 Budget, the indirect tax revenue to GDP ratio is also expected to be virtually unchanged over the projection period, with growth in sales tax and petroleum excise duty revenue being almost fully offset by the reductions in collections of customs duty associated with the tariff reduction programme. The narrowing of the indirect tax base through growth of the lower taxed services sector and slow growth in alcohol and tobacco consumption are other factors limiting growth in indirect tax revenue.

The States' aggregate (underlying general government) budget balance is projected to improve from an estimated deficit of 0.3 per cent of GDP in FY 1994/95[43] to small surpluses in FY 1996/97 and FY 1997/98. This amelioration reflects a fall in outlays as a percentage of GDP which more than offsets that in revenue. The main factors contributing to the decline in outlays are, as a share of GDP, reductions in: subsidies, loans and grants to public trading and financial enterprises; expenditure on capital works; and termination payments as well as on-going savings generated by public sector reform programmes (particularly in

48

the area of wages and salaries costs). With respect to revenue, which also falls in real terms, around one half of the projected decline as a percentage of GDP is attributable to lower own-source revenue. This mainly reflects lower dividends from State-owned trading enterprises, slow growth in franchise fee revenue from alcohol and tobacco consumption and in property taxes. None of these factors represents either a reduction in the States' revenue raising effort or a reduction in the States' capacity to raise revenue. The rest of the decline in revenue as a percentage of GDP is attributable to a decline in Commonwealth grants to States, which also decline in real terms. The real decline in grants primarily reflects the winding down of a number of projects supported by the Commonwealth through specific purpose payments to States; general purpose payments to the States are assumed to be maintained in real per capita terms until FY 1996/97.

General government net debt is projected to peak in 1995 and 1996 at 28 per cent of GDP and to decline slightly in subsequent years; these debt levels are considerably higher than those of the late 1980s, when net debt fell to a low of 11 per cent of GDP[44] (Diagram 20). This outlook reflects the stabilisation of net

Diagram 20. **GENERAL GOVERNMENT NET INDEBTEDNESS**[1]

Fiscal years starting July, as per cent of GDP

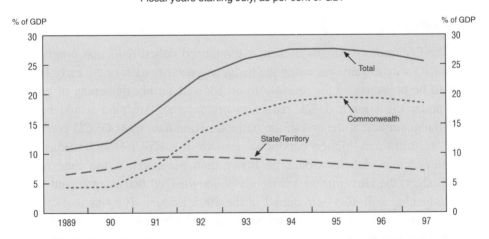

1. Net debt projections are approximate only and are calculated by adding the deficit (including asset sales) to the year's stock of debt.
Source: National Fiscal Outlook, 1995.

49

government debt as a percentage of GDP for the Commonwealth by FY 1995/96 and declines for States throughout the projection period.

The stance of fiscal policy

OECD estimates indicate that approximately four-fifths of the deterioration in the underlying general government budget balance between 1990 and 1994 was structural. On a calendar-year basis, the cyclically-adjusted budget deficit increased by approximately $4\frac{1}{2}$ per cent of GDP over this period, leaving a structural deficit of $4\frac{1}{4}$ per cent of GDP. This increase is estimated to reflect to a similar extent both higher expenditure and lower revenue. On the basis of present policies, including the foreshadowed acceleration in the Commonwealth consolidation programme to be incorporated in the 1995 Budget, the OECD projects on a calendar-year basis that the underlying general government budget deficit will decline as a percentage of GDP from 4.6 per cent in 1994 to 1.3 per cent in 1996; on a fiscal-year basis, the deficit is projected to fall to 1.9 per cent of GDP in FY 1995/96, compared with 2.1-2.3 per cent of GDP in the NFO 1995 projections.[45] Approximately three-quarters of the projected reduction in the general government budget deficit is estimated to be attributable to non-cyclical factors, predominantly lower expenditure as a percentage of GDP. The structural deficit is projected to fall to around $1\frac{1}{2}$ per cent of GDP by 1996.

Assessment

The Commonwealth government's announced deficit reduction programme goes a long way towards reversing the budgetary deterioration of the early 1990s, and will be bolstered by the recently foreshadowed further tightening of policy. Even under the current deficit reduction programme, Australia would have a lower budget deficit at the end of the outlook period than most OECD countries. However, although higher economic growth for FY 1994/95 means that no-policy-change deficits would be lower than projected at the time of the 1994 Budget, the Government has rightly acknowledged that a significant structural tightening will also be required in the 1995 Budget. The risk that cyclical improvement to the projections may not be sustainable in later years emphasises the need for reductions in projected structural deficits. In view of the medium-term implications of increasing public debt and low levels of public saving. it is important that lasting improvements to the budgetary position be achieved.

While net general government debt as a percentage of GDP remains lower in Australia than in most other OECD countries, the projected increase over the present economic cycle, from around 11 per cent in 1989 to a projected peak of 27 per cent in 1995 and 1996 (and then falling), underlines the importance of medium-term fiscal policy objectives; the announced acceleration in the deficit reduction programme will, of course, assist in stabilising public debt at a lower level than currently projected. However, given the need for Australia to bolster national saving in order to finance its investment requirements, policy should continue to have in mind the need to prevent public indebtedness notching up from one cycle to the next, as some other OECD countries have experienced. This would contribute to lower net external liabilities than otherwise.

Australia's net external liabilities are relatively high, at around 55 per cent of GDP in mid-1994. Debt makes up approximately 70 per cent of these liabilities. Net external liabilities have increased markedly since the beginning of the 1980s, when they were 23 per cent of GDP, as has the proportion of liabilities which is debt. Probably mainly reflecting the increase in external debt, Australia's credit rating was downgraded in the mid-1980s to Aa2/AA, adding a risk premium to interest rates for Australian borrowers; this premium was estimated to add $1/4$ to $1/2$ percentage point to the interest rates which the Commonwealth government had to pay on US dollar borrowings in mid-1993.[46] Were net external debt to go on rising, this could affect credit ratings and investor sentiment and expose the economy to greater risks of instability. For an economy subject to large swings in its terms of trade, a low public debt policy, which would contribute to lower external debt, would appear to be prudent in helping to avoid the possible need for sharp policy adjustments. And in view of the future public expenditure commitments associated with an ageing population structure, vigorous action to increase public saving over the next two decades will probably be required if high levels of public debt are subsequently to be avoided.

The need to ensure that the economy grows at a sustainable rate provides an ideal opportunity to start increasing public savings on a long-term basis. And fiscal policy is likely to be more effective than monetary policy in slowing growth in aggregate demand in the short term, especially if fiscal measures involve a reduction in the structural deficit; structural measures are likely to have a greater effect on aggregate demand growth than temporary measures as they are less likely to be offset by lower private savings. Unless there is the political will to cut government programmes, the emphasis in reducing the structural deficit is likely to have to be on increasing taxes, which have declined structurally since the late 1980s. In view of the low growth in the indirect tax base, widening this base is an option which would be worth considering.

III. Progress in structural reform

Microeconomic reforms continue to play a decisive role in the government's strategy for improving the conditions for sustainable higher economic growth and bringing the rate of unemployment down to 5 per cent by the turn of the century. Given that recent national estimates put the non-accelerating-inflation rate of unemployment (NAIRU) at around 7 per cent,[47] the attainment of the unemployment goal requires the reduction of the "equilibrium level" of unemployment by a substantial amount. The government's strategy in this regard is to foster the functioning of the labour market through gradual but continuing reform of industrial relations and a range of labour-market measures laid out in the White Paper entitled *Working Nation*. This chapter discusses these reform efforts as well as major recent initiatives to stimulate competition in sectors which are largely sheltered from foreign competition.

Industrial relations: the move from centralised to enterprise bargaining

The objectives of reform

The on-going reform of the industrial relations system aims at extending the scope for more flexible[48] and productive workplaces. The reform is guided by the – now generally accepted – recognition that higher flexibility and productivity of enterprises can be achieved by moving away from the traditional centrally-determined awards[49] system of industrial relations towards increased reliance on bargaining of wages and other work conditions at the company level. The Prices and Incomes Accord, based on the central award system, delivered real wage flexibility at the macroeconomic level and contributed to strong employment growth in the 1980s. However, in view of the need to adapt the industrial relations system to the requirements of the 1990s, the Accord has evolved so as to provide a supportive environment for the shift towards enterprise bargaining.[50] Less resort to arbitration by the Australian Industrial Relations Commission (AIRC) and more responsibility of industrial parties for their own relations is expected to strengthen the direct link between labour compensation and productivity at the workplace, which should help in keeping inflationary pressures low. It should also help improve the efficiency of the existing capital stock and the quality of new investment for which scope probably remains in Australia even after allowing for some recent apparent improvement (Diagram 21).

Certified enterprise agreements

A move towards more decentralised industrial relations began in 1987,[51] when the Conciliation and Arbitration Commission (the precursor of the AIRC) of the time awarded wage increases which were linked in part to productivity improvements negotiated at the enterprise level. So-called *certified agreements,* which were introduced by the 1988 *Industrial Relations Act,* were intended to enable individual firms and trade unions to negotiate agreements on wages and work conditions notwithstanding the central wage fixing principles as long as the

Diagram 21. **INVESTMENT SHARE AND TOTAL FACTOR PRODUCTIVITY**
Business sector, 1984-93

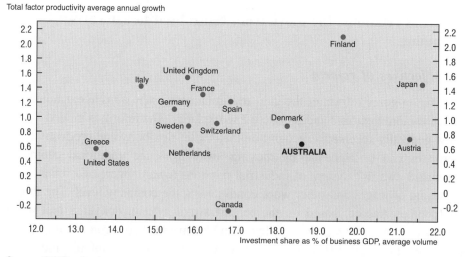

Total factor productivity average annual growth

Investment share as % of business GDP, average volume

Source: OECD estimates.

AIRC considered the agreements to be consistent with the "public interest". Provisions were also made for multi-employer certified agreements. But the specific rules developed by the AIRC to conclude and register certified agreements turned out to be rather cumbersome in practice and thereby of only limited attractiveness for social partners, so that bargaining at the enterprise level spread only slowly. In consequence, the *Industrial Relations Act* was amended in July 1992 so as to streamline the ratification procedure for such agreements. The most notable simplification by the amended *Act* is the replacement of the "public interest" clause by the requirement for an agreement to entail no worsening in the package of total entitlement (the "no disadvantage test", see below). This represents a significant reduction in the role of the AIRC. The public interest test was retained for multi-employer certified agreements.

Although the amended *Act* clearly facilitated workplace bargaining between trade unions and firms or industries, the role assigned to unions in the procedure of registering a certified agreement probably discouraged non-unionised enterprises from adopting enterprise bargaining: in order to get a negotiated enterprise agreement ratified as legally binding with the AIRC, it was necessary for constitutional reasons to prove the existence of an interstate dispute, which for companies operating in one state was difficult to achieve without involving a union.

Enterprise flexibility agreements

A further step towards workplace bargaining was made on 30 March 1994, when the *Industrial Relations Reform Act 1993* became law. The *Reform Act* includes – *inter alia* – provisions for *enterprise flexibility agreements* which allow corporations, including "non-unionised" and "partly unionised" companies with federal award coverage[52] to reach agreements directly with employees, provided that a majority of employees approve the agreement. There is no requirement for an inter-state dispute to exist. In the case of non-unionised corporations, there is no requirement for any union to be notified about the agreement, although hearing dates for applications for the approval of EFA's are made public by the AIRC, and unions with award coverage at the enterprise have a right to be heard at the Commission hearing. In the case of firms with partly unionised workforces, unions with members and relevant award coverage have to be informed at the beginning of enterprise negotiations and must be given the opportunity to take part in negotiations and to agree to be bound by the final agreement. Unions with award coverage have a right to be heard at the AIRC hearing.

The central award system remains in place, which is considered as an advantage by the Government as it allows parties to make only the change they perceive necessary, while keeping intact those award matters with which they are satisfied. Hence, where an agreement is silent on a matter, the award provision applies. The Government's recent legislative reforms include provisions aimed at simplifying the federal award system and making awards more flexible and relevant to the workplace, thus encouraging the better tailoring of working arrangements to the circumstances of particular workplaces. To this end, the AIRC has established a process to review all federal awards on a three-yearly basis to identify and remedy any deficiencies, such as obsolete and unnecessarily detailed provisions, while retaining their minimum safety net function.

The AIRC is required to make proposed *certified agreements* or *enterprise flexibility agreements* subject to a "no disadvantage test". The prevailing interpretation of the test's meaning is that it allows individual award conditions to be altered, provided that employees are not disadvantaged with regard to their terms and conditions taken *as a whole*.[53] There appears, however, the risk that the AIRC assesses the overall merits of a proposed agreement less favourably than the negotiating parties and that this could then induce the *Commission* to refuse the ratification of an agreement. This could occur, for example, if both employers and employees deem it desirable to let working conditions fall below award provisions in exchange for wage increases. However, it should be noted that a large number of agreements that reduce some award conditions in return for improvements in wages and other conditions have already been certified or approved by the AIRC.

The Government expects the new *Reform Act* to speed up the spread of enterprise agreements, which was somewhat disappointing until 1993. The government's target is that 80 per cent of the labour force under federal awards be covered by direct bargains before the end of 1996. Around 3 240 enterprise agreements have been finalised by the AIRC up to the end of January 1995. These arrangements cover an estimated 1.4 million employees, representing around 57 per cent of workers in the federal award system. The pace of bargaining has clearly accelerated with the number of agreements increasing by around 1 475 in 1994 compared to an increase of around 1 020 in 1993.

The States

The States have the constitutional power to legislate directly on wages. During the period of centralisation the State Industrial Relations Commissions also conducted wage cases and handed down decisions on adjustments to awards, generally along the lines of the federal Commission's decisions (and continue to do so under the more decentralised system). In recent years, States have changed their systems also to encourage enterprise bargaining. Some States have followed the federal pattern; for example, Queensland's Industrial Reform Act of March 1994 largely mirrors the Commonwealth legislation, including a no disadvantage test and the introduction of enterprise flexibility agreements into the State-award system. South Australia's Employee and Industrial Relations Act of May 1994 gives employees freedom of association and encourages workplace agreements and enterprise bargaining while offering a safety net of minimum conditions to employees. New South Wales and Tasmania have also introduced legislation that allows enterprise bargaining without union involvement. But by far the most fundamental change took place in Victoria, where individual and collective contracts replaced awards already in October 1992. However, the impact of State reforms of industrial relations is difficult to assess owing to a lack of data.[54] It should also be noted that bargaining does occur outside the formalised industrial relations system, resulting in unregistered (informal) agreements. Smaller firms in particular may seek to avoid involvement with the unions and may therefore eschew *formal* enterprise bargaining. Currently about one-fifth of wage and salary earners is estimated to be award-free.

Assessment

All told, "the Industrial Relations Reform Act 1993 ... has introduced the most sweeping changes to the federal industrial (relations) system since its inception in 1904".[55] But the new legislation still remains very complex[56] and highly prescriptive for both certified agreements and enterprise flexibility agreements. This may mean that negotiating enterprise agreements is time consuming and costly. Nevertheless, the Government's view is that the procedural requirements provide important protection for employees. Apart from this issue, the implementation of the legislation so far has not been trouble-free largely because it left scope for different interpretation as to the extent of involvement by the AIRC as well as by trade unions.[57] However, there have been several key cases before the AIRC in which the interpretation of some of the new provisions of the legislation has been a key issue. Decisions in these cases are expected to establish precedents for both the parties and the AIRC in future.

In addition, there is the question as to whether awards are best suited to perform a safety-net function. Although most industries have one award which covers the majority of employees, there are numerous other awards referring to particular occupations and crafts.[58] Hence, there are in effect several safety nets underpinning agreements, and the minimum rates of pay as laid down in awards result in a network of minimum wages. Some argue that because these complex safety-net structures encompass matters beyond basic standards they may constrain the capacity of the labour force to adjust to change. Besides, these safety-net minimum wages do not apply only to low-paid workers, so that they are hard to defend on social grounds. The A$ 8 per week pay rises made available in Accord VII are also criticised on the grounds that they can apply to employees who receive relatively high minimum rates of pay.[59] Such critics argue that from a social and practical point of view a simpler approach to protect the low-paid would have been to legislate a minimum hourly wage and standards regarding basic work conditions applicable to all workers with certain exceptions which could be justified, for example, to encourage the training of youth. On the other hand, the view of others, including the Government, is that a secure safety net to underpin enterprise bargaining is important not only on social justice grounds, but also to secure the success of enterprise bargaining, by enhancing the level of trust and co-operation between workers and employers and making sure that the focus of bargaining is on productivity improvements.

The Working Nation labour market initiatives

Purpose of the programme

Microeconomic reform in combination with sound macroeconomic policies will eventually boost aggregate output. But the beneficial effects on the labour market will probably show with a substantial lag. This is the more so if downward flexibility of wages is deemed socially unacceptable, as appears to be the case in Australia.[60] Moreover, the experience from the 1983-86 expansion suggests that, in the absence of supplementary measures, the long-term unemployed tend to gain far less from the employment-creating effects of buoyant economic activity than do new entrants or re-entrants to the labour force or short-term unemployed (Diagram 22). Empirical studies indicate that in Australia a person who was unemployed for less than three months has more than twice the chance of finding a job than a person without work for between one and two years and four times the chance of a person unemployed for two years or more.[61] In part, employers seem to use the duration of unemployment as a screening device to sort out potential hires. This is in line with the observation that long-term unemployed as a group frequently suffer from poor education,[62] low skills and insufficient experience; there are reports that many employers are unwilling even to interview them.[63]

Against this background, the Government launched a comprehensive employment programme[64] which, through an emphasis on the formation of skills, tries to ensure that long-term unemployed benefit more from the economic recovery (Box 1). The approach of the programme is in line with findings that in order to enhance the effectiveness[65] of active labour-market programmes, they should be targeted on specific client groups, or be designed to remedy specific

Diagram 22. **TOTAL AND LONG-TERM UNEMPLOYMENT**

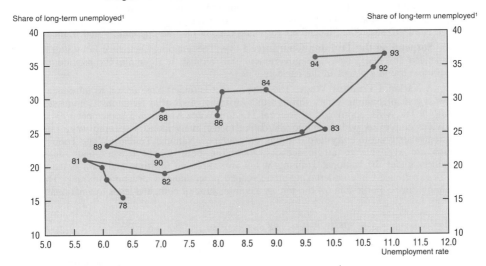

1. Unemployed for one year and over as a per cent of all unemployed.
Source: Australian Bureau of Statistics and OECD.

Box 1.   Major initiatives under the Working Nation programme

A Job Compact. It provides individual case management and access to a range of labour market programmes leading to offer of a job placement for all people aged 18 years and over who have been receiving unemployment income support or allowances for at least 18 months. Job placements include subsidised private sector jobs where a wage subsidy of between A$ 100 and A$ 230 is paid per week for a period of 13 to 26 weeks, depending on the classification of the unemployed jobseeker. In addition, a bonus will be paid to employers who retain their workers three months after the subsidy ends. At the end of the Job Compact, intensive job search assistance is provided.

Non Job-Compact Assistance. The Government is committed to assisting all unemployed and will maintain and improve current labour-market assistance to non-Job Compact unemployed. It also targets assistance to those most at risk of becoming long-term unemployed. Case management is also available to non Job Compact clients who are assessed at high risk of becoming long-term unemployed, or who have been in receipt of unemployment income support or allowances for 12 months or more. Additional funding for this purpose is A$ 2 billion (cumulatively) over the next four years (not including the Youth Training Initiative).

A Youth Training Initiative (YTI). Unemployed people under the age of 18 are provided with case management assistance to find suitable work, training or education placement, rather than remaining out of work. Young people participating in the YTI will be paid a Youth Training Allowance (YTA), which will replace the Job Search Allowance. Those young people registering as unemployed on or after 1 January 1995 will be affected by the YTI. Funding for the YTI will be a cumulative A$ 711 million over the next four years including the YTA.

Expansion in Entry-level Training Places. The Government is committed to provide a minimum of 50 000 additional entry-level training places by FY 1995/96. This expansion of places over four years will cost approximately A$ 770 million. To this end, the system of payments to employers for providing young people with training place will be revised* to strengthen incentives for enterprises to take on apprentices and trainees.

Suspending the Training Guarantee Levy. The Training Guarantee Levy will be suspended for two years. The government will abolish it if employers provide the additional training places in the package.

A National Training Wage. The government is undertaking action to introduce a new system of training wages through the Australian Industrial Relations Commission (AIRC). The AIRC approved the National Training Wage Award on 5 September 1994. It provides employers with a simple alternative to the many industry-specific wage rates currently applying to entry-level training programmes. National Training Wage Traineeships are available to all jobseekers, including both school leavers and adults. Trainees under the National Training Wage are employed full-time and gain practical work experience while undertaking an accredited programme of structural training. This training can be on-the-job, off-the-job, or a combination of both, and leads to a nationally

---

*   *Cf.* Working Nation (1994), *Policies and programs, op. cit.,* Box 4.6, p. 101.

(Continued on next page)

recognised qualification. Employers may also be eligible for training subsidies to help them meet the cost of hiring a trainee. The amount of training subsidy an employer receives depends on the type of training being provided and how long the job seeker has been unemployed. The White Paper allocated A$ 54.3 million for traineeship arrangements in FY 1994/95. This will provide 33 600 traineeship places, including those covered by the National Training Wage, the Australian Traineeship System and Career Start Traineeships.

NETTFORCE. It is the task of the newly-established National Employment and Training Taskforce (NETTFORCE) to encourage employers to offer additional entry-level training places and Job Compact places. NETTFORCE aims to facilitate the implementation of the national training wage by promoting the speedy recognition of training packages across Australia. Once recognised, these training packages can be used by employers to train people employed under the National Training Wage. To achieve its aims, NETTFORCE is establishing Industry Training Companies (ITCs) in a range of industries. NETTFORCE has been allocated A$ 1 million over four years for administrative costs, with additional funds for the establishment of the ITCs.

Restructuring Income Support Arrangements. Incentives for recipients of social security payments (including unemployment income support) to seek additional income are to be improved by lowering the withdrawal rate for benefits from a dollar to 70 cents for each additional dollar earned, and introducing income testing eligibility for entitlements on an individual basis with the spouse income test applying only if the partner has substantial income.

Developing the transition from School to Work. To forge closer links between industry and schools, an Australian Student Traineeship Foundation will be established. Its task will be to develop and support national upper secondary school-industry vocational training programmes. The Foundation will be funded at a cost of A$ 38 million over the next four years.

Improved Delivery of Employment and Training Services. The Commonwealth Employment Service (CES) will be restructured in relation to the provision of case management services and these services will be opened to competition to provide a more effective and responsive service to both employers and the unemployed. Case Management is the means by which long-term unemployed jobseekers and those assessed as at "high risk" of becoming long-term unemployed will receive employment and training assistance in future. In order to respond more effectively to regional and local needs and priorities in employment and training, the government will establish up to 60 Area Consultative Committees (ACCs). They will include local business, union, government, CES and community representatives. The ACCs will ensure that CES services and programmes are responsive to local needs and complement regional development initiatives.

Other measures. These include *New Work Opportunities* projects (publicly funded community based projects involving substantive work experience and training in areas where employment opportunities are limited), a national literacy survey and income support measures targeted at key client groups such as Aboriginal and Torres Strait Islander peoples, people with disabilities and migrants.

labour market problems;[66] programmes which are too broadly defined are likely to yield disappointing results. While building upon the most successful elements of existing labour market programmes, the Government's latest measures involve a far more comprehensive strategy of active labour market assistance with close linkages with education, training and skill-enhancing measures than has ever been attempted in Australia.

The *Working Nation* employment programme is estimated to raise Commonwealth outlays (net of savings in social security expenditure) by a cumulative A$ 6.5 billion above previous projections over four years (Table 11). In the first *full* year of its operation (FY 1995/96) the package will add A$ 1.7 billion to Commonwealth outlays – about one-third of a per cent of

Table 11. **Net fiscal cost of Working Nation measures**

A$ million

	Estimated impact on outlays			
	1994/95	1995/96	1996/97	1997/98
Outlays				
Employment and training				
Job compact	538.1	911.4	1 030.5	960.9
Entry level training	72.7	134.5	138.3	179.1
Youth	34.2	71.3	86.9	87.4
Measures for women	0.0	5.1	18.2	26.2
Measures for Aboriginal and Torres Strait Islander people	6.8	12.6	22.2	27.7
Measures for people with a disability	7.3	7.9	7.8	7.7
Improved delivery of labour market assistance	149.6	29.0	–0.3	3.0
Other related measures	63.0	74.0	64.8	52.6
Sub-total employment and training	871.7	1 245.7	1 368.4	1 344.6
Income support	37.2	278.5	270.1	293.1
Industry	71.4	100.3	113.4	106.5
Regional development	35.7	52.9	93.2	81.1
Science	31.3	37.2	42.5	47.1
Trade	19.2	19.1	18.7	14.8
Total outlays	1 066.5	1 733.8	1 906.3	1 887.2
Savings in social security expenditure	–7.8	–8.1	–18.2	–17.6
Total cost	1 058.7	1 725.7	1 888.1	1 869.6

Source: Commonwealth of Australia, *Working Nation, Policies and Programs,* Canberra, May 1994.

GDP – while it will cost some A$ 1 billion in the current year (FY 1994/95). The bulk of the spending is assigned to measures of various types aimed at the promotion of "employment and training", amounting to gross outlays of A$ 2.1 billion in FY 1995/96, which are expected to be offset by savings of about A$ 800 million in unemployment allowances. In addition, nearly A$ 500 million are to be spent in FY 1995/96 on new income support measures (A$ 280 million), industry, science and trade initiatives (A$ 160 million) and specific regional development programmes (A$ 50 million).

The centre-piece of the package is the *Job Compact,* in particular the offer of a job for 6 to 12 months. The job placement will be either an unsubsidised or subsidised job with a private or public sector employer; a self-employment opportunity; or a job with a publicly funded environment or community project involving work experience and/or training.[67] Altogether, *Job Compact* is expected to cost around A$ 1 billion per year (net of saved social security benefit payments) and hence to account for a little over half of the total (net) cost of the entire package.

The *Job Compact* programme focuses on persons in receipt of unemployment income support for at least 18 months. This is based on the notion that taking those from the back of the unemployment queue and giving them training and some work experience will keep them in touch with the workplace and with required skills. In this way the programme is expected to improve economic efficiency and equity at the same time. There is a reciprocal obligation on these people to accept a reasonable offer of employment or training (Table 12). The

Table 12. **Reciprocal obligation: non-payment penalty periods**[1]

	Period for which allowance is not paid		
	Unemployed for less than 12 months	Unemployed for 12 months and less than 18 months	Unemployed for 18 months or more
First breach	2 weeks	4 weeks	6 weeks
Second and subsequent breach	6 weeks plus most recent previous penalty	6 weeks plus most recent previous penalty	6 weeks plus most recent previous penalty

1.   This table shows the revised non-payment penalty periods for breaches of the activity test.
Source: Commonwealth of Australia, *Working Nation, Policies and Programs,* Canberra, May 1994.

Job Compact has been introduced progressively from July 1994 onward, and over half a million unemployed people are expected to be individually case-managed over the next four years

One of the objectives of the *Job Compact* is to lower wage pressures by increasing the efficiency of the labour market. Wage pressures could be reduced by the strengthening of the competitive powers of the long-term unemployed ("outsiders") and – in consequence – lowering the bargaining powers of job-holders ("insiders"). It would materialise if the *Job Compact* made the long-term unemployed a more effective part of the labour force and prepared them better to fill job vacancies as they arise (enhanced job-matching efficiency). As a consequence, critical wage pressures which require restrictive macroeconomic policies would emerge at a lower rate of unemployment than hitherto, thereby allowing a higher level of output to be attained.

Another route to higher potential output is to increase the marginal productivity of the unemployed through education and training and other skill-enhancing measures, which could then improve aggregate labour productivity. This strategy lies behind the training and education elements of the *Working Nation* programme, together with the introduction of training wages, which addresses the inappropriateness of the current award-wage setting for job seekers with low or outdated skills.[68] Rates of pay under the National Training Wage reflect the skill levels of the employees and the requirement that employers provide training. These measures, in combination with other more broad-ranging education and training measures outside the *Working Nation* package, are designed to raise the skills of the workforce in the longer term, thereby addressing ongoing concerns with the adequacy of Australia's skill base to meet its future labour needs.

Another key part of the employment package is a set of changes in income support arrangements, effective as from 1 July 1995, which are expected to cost on average some A$ 280 million per year. The changes aim at minimising the adverse effect of the so-called "poverty trap" (or "dependency trap") on labour supply. Such a "trap" arises at low income levels when the interaction of taxation and the withdrawal of social benefits result in no or very little additional disposable income from extra work. The changed system will ease the financial penalties associated hitherto with the taking of part-time or temporary jobs[69] and ensure that any financial disadvantage tapers in more gradually and at higher hours of work. To this end, unemployed couples are to be individually entitled to their half of income support with spouse income below A$ 231 per week not affecting the entitlement. A parenting allowance will be introduced for those spouses who cannot be expected to seek gainful work because of parenting responsibilities. Partner allowance will continue for spouses aged over 40 and without dependent children, provided the spouse has no recent workforce experience (*i.e.,* has not been employed for more than 20 hours a week for a total of 13 weeks or more during the last 12 months). The standard allowance income test will be modified to replace the dollar-for-dollar withdrawal rate with a 70 per cent rate. This should help encouraging part-time work because an unemployed person will gain financially from taking up work. As a result of this change, the government estimates that 33 000 unemployed people will get part-time work and some of the 132 000 people doing some part-time work will increase their incomes by working more.

Assessment

The *Working Nation* package will, in a relatively efficient way, help ease the difficulties the long-term unemployed have experienced in obtaining a job. These initiatives are an important element of the Government's strategy to bring the unemployment rate down to 5 per cent over the next five years. The overall impact of the *Working Nation* employment package on the labour market will depend importantly on the quality of its design and implementation. In the short term, the impact of the measures on unemployment will depend on the size of the so-called displacement effects (where a job provided by a labour market programme targeted at a particular group may be at the expense of a job elsewhere) and deadweight costs (where labour market programmes subsidise new jobs which would have been created anyway). In the longer term, well-designed labour market programmes will bring positive returns if they increase the effectiveness of the long-term unemployed in searching for and obtaining work, thereby reducing wage pressures and the NAIRU. The size of these effects is an empirical question which will need to be evaluated carefully.

While the employment package builds on the most successful elements of existing labour market programmes, a number of the measures introduced are untested and hence will need to be monitored closely. For example, public works programmes such as the New Work Opportunities need to be carefully designed to ensure that the benefits to recipients in terms of work experience and improved self-esteem are not outweighed by any possible stigmatising effects of participating in these programmes. It is important in this context that these work placements provide long-lasting work skills which are relevant to market demands. Given the large scale and innovative nature of the labour market and training programme commitments in *Working Nation,* it is appropriate that the Government is putting in place a comprehensive strategy for the evaluation of these measures.

The changes to social security arrangements which will remove some of the disincentives for the unemployed to take low-paid and/or part-time work can be expected to assist in reducing the NAIRU. Prior to the July 1995 changes to the income test, allowees faced effective marginal tax rates (EMTRs) of around 100 per cent and ranging up to approximately 110 per cent. Under the changes that will come into effect (July 1995), EMTRs will be reduced. A family with one income earner and a non working partner with two children will face an EMTR below 80 per cent for the income range A\$ 70-A\$ 225. From around A\$ 230 per week to around A\$ 380 per week, the EMTR will rise to approximately 90 per cent. At private income levels below A\$ 70 per week, the EMTRs range from about 30-63 per cent. Extra costs associated with attending work such as travel and clothing may act as additional disincentives for relatively low-skilled recipients of unemployment allowances, although they remain eligible for family payments after entering low income employment.

Other structural reform projects

As policies complementary to the reform of industrial relations and the new labour market initiatives, the *Working Nation* programme touches upon a variety of other microeconomic reform projects,[70] all of which aim at the removal of impediments to competition and at the creation of conditions conducive to better enterprise performance. The measures range from the – already adopted – tariff reform and financial market deregulation to regional policies and waterfront, shipping and aviation reform.[71] Some of the initiatives are completely new while others are based on earlier reform projects which have not yet been put into practice, such as the recommendations of the Committee of Inquiry into National Competition Policy[72] (the "Hilmer Committee").

The "Hilmer reforms"

Exposing sheltered enterprises of the public and private sector to more competition has been identified by the Hilmer Committee Report as a major avenue to higher productivity and growth. To this end, the Report suggests applying the *Trade Practices Act*, Australia's main competition policy statute, universally to all business activity in Australia, hence extending its application to Government Business Enterprises (GBE), Statutory Marketing Authorities – the main source of assistance to agriculture – and unincorporated associations. The Report also proposes new policy guidelines to build a more competitive economy, particularly where the lack of competitive pressures is a result of government regulation or government ownership. These include the review of regulatory restrictions to competition, structural reform of public monopolies, the granting of access rights to essential facilities (such as telecommunications networks, electricity grids and rail networks), prices oversight of Government Business Enterprises and ensuring that public and private enterprises compete on equal terms. The Report proposes the repeal of many government regulations which impede the functioning of markets unless it can be clearly demonstrated that particular restrictions are in the public interest.

The Council of Australian Governments (COAG), which consists of representatives of the Commonwealth and each of the State and Territory governments, endorsed the thrust of the Hilmer-Report recommendations at its meeting in February 1994, and at its August 1994 meeting, it agreed – in principle – on a package of competition policy reforms and transitional arrangements.[73] While the Hilmer Committee noted that the Commonwealth could implement most of the Report's recommendations unilaterally, the Committee favoured the Commonwealth adopting a co-operative approach with State and Territory governments to implement the reforms. The Commonwealth decided to adopt the co-operative approach which will require the States and Territories passing legislation applying the competitive conduct rules to persons in their jurisdictions. The States and Territories will also be asked to sign intergovernmental agreements to apply agreed competition principles in their jurisdictions. However, the Commonwealth has signalled that it is prepared to implement the reforms unilaterally if it fails to get the support of the States and Territories at the April 1995 COAG meeting, so as to bring new arrangements into effect by mid-1995. At the August 1994 COAG meeting, it was agreed that all governments should share the benefits to economic growth and revenue from the Hilmer and related reforms. The Industry Commission has been asked to asses the benefits and this assessment will be one of the matters considered at the April 1995 COAG meeting.

The first practical change ensuing from the new national approach to competition policy is the agreement of COAG at its February 1994 meeting to a national gas market by July 1996, which will clear intrastate and interstate trade in gas from regulatory barriers, ensure third party access to networks on non-discriminatory terms and pave the way for increased commercialisation of publicly-owned gas utilities. At the same meeting, the COAG endorsed a strategic framework for the efficient and sustainable reform of the Australian water industry – including cost-based pricing for water services and more widespread trading in entitlements – and agreed to its implementation. A progress report on implementation is to be provided to the first COAG meeting in 1995, with further progress reports to be prepared annually over the following four years. Heads of State government have also agreed that a competitive electricity market will commence on 1 July 1995, with an independent transmission network and competitive generation. Of the States, Victoria is the most advanced in the separation of electricity generation, transmission and distribution activities. It has established five separate distribution companies, a transmission company, a wholesale exchange company, and more recently, separated its generation utility into five units which trade independently. Other States involved in the initial competitive electricity market have either separated their generation and transmission units or plan to do so before the competitive market commences.

Competitive features have been introduced into the telecommunications sector, and in 1997 the present limits on entry to the telecommunications market will expire. A telecommunications policy review is now under way to determine the regulatory framework that will apply after 1997, when open competition will replace the present managed duopoly between Telecom, which is government owned, and a second licensed carrier, Optus, which is privately owned and already competes on mobile, long distance and international calls. The principles of the new national competition policy will be taken into consideration as part of the disposal of the Federal Airport Corporation's airports. The Government will establish a regulatory structure which will protect the public interest and be sensitive to requirements associated with the leasehold sales.

Government purchasing

The Government is in the process of restructuring its procurement guide-lines so that its role as a major purchaser of goods and services can more directly foster the capabilities of Australian suppliers, without compromising on quality and price. The revised policy will establish a closer link between government purchasing and industry development. This will help to overcome a perceived reluctance to purchase from Australian suppliers and a lack of knowledge of the capabilities of these suppliers. Suppliers for large government contracts will be expected to demonstrate a commitment to fostering Australian industry develop-ment. Great care will have to be taken that by putting stronger emphasis on Australian industry development, the new initiative will not harm the quality of public services, strain government budgets and give wrong signals to domestic suppliers. However, experience has demonstrated that value for money and effective purchasing outcomes are not diminished, and can be enhanced, by dealing with local companies, thus providing opportunities for local industry development. The Government expects that it generally will not have to pay a premium for acceptable industry development outcomes.

Shipping and waterfront

Empirical estimates point to strong productivity gains in the maritime sector in recent years, as a result of increased workplace flexibility and the adoption of "world best practice" management operations. For example, stevedoring charges fell by some 24 per cent between 1990 and 1993, crane handling rates increased remarkably between 1989 and 1993 (nearly 50 per cent) and the average crew levels of the Australian fleet declined steadily. However, in a recent coastal shipping benchmark exercise, the *Bureau of Industry Economics* (1994) con-cluded that notwithstanding the substantial labour reforms implemented in the industry a sizeable competitive gap remains between Australian and some inter-national operations. Manning costs have been identified as the main contributor to the comparative cost gap. The Government is considering further measures to reduce this gap.

A major problem is that at present, seafarers are employed on an industry basis rather than by individual companies. They are recruited through an industry selection process to a labour pool (the "roster"), allocated to ships from the roster and returned to that roster if discharged from the ship. Replacing this pool system with company employment could significantly increase labour productivity through more flexible and efficient use of labour. Company employment would, through the introduction of enterprise bargaining, allow negotiation of more competitive work practices tailored to the needs of individual shipping lines and their employees. However, as part of an agreement with the Government (September 1994), the unions agreed to consider the negotiation of an industrial reform package, including further reductions in crew sizes and crew to berth ratios, changing employment arrangements so that costs would match those under company employment, a long term wage agreement and reductions in training costs. For its part, the Government agreed to investigate a number of changes to taxation arrangements which would reduce the cost disadvantage of Australian shipping.

IV. The health-care system

Introduction

Over recent decades the health status of Australians has improved significantly, helped by the health-care system which guarantees universal coverage and yields a large measure of satisfaction among the population at a reasonable overall cost to the economy. Nonetheless, in common with other OECD countries, health-care expenditures have grown rapidly, with their GDP share increasing from 4.9 per cent in 1960 to 8.5 per cent in 1993, close to the OECD average. Whereas such growth for most other goods and services might be interpreted as a sign that the market system is working effectively to reallocate resources to their most valued uses, the same is unlikely to be true for health care. Markets for health care are subject to important information failures which tend to result in pressures for the over-provision of medical services (see Box 2). Governments in most OECD countries, including Australia, counter these pressures through various forms of restraint on public health-care expenditure.

Australia, like most other OECD countries, has emphasised "top-down" approaches to restraining growth in health expenditures. The main planks in this strategy have been to cap budgets for public-sector hospitals and to restrain price increases for medical services and pharmaceutical goods. These were the main avenues open to the government under current institutional arrangements in the health-care sector. This approach now needs to be supplemented with more sophisticated incentives for efficient production of hospital services. A number of States have now introduced casemix funding arrangements and the initial results in Victoria have been very promising. The Commonwealth has signalled its intention to incorporate casemix measures to an increasing extent in its financial agreements with the States. Much work remains to be done to provide incentives for quality and consumer focus to balance the incentives for efficiency that are provided by casemix funding. Furthermore, Australia will have to find ways of restraining health expenditure in those parts of the system that are uncapped. Otherwise it will face an acceleration in health expenditures and/or a deterioration in the quality of health care. The main alternatives for restraining health expenditure are likely to focus on influencing the behaviour of service providers, funders and consumers alike by offering a better pattern of incentives. Particular attention needs to be paid to reducing the incentives for the over-supply of medical services and on empowering purchasers of health care to obtain better value for their expenditures.

The chapter begins with a brief description of institutional arrangements for health care in Australia, with particular emphasis on the incentives facing the different participants in the sector. Australia's health outcomes and aggregate expenditure trends are compared with those of other OECD countries in the next two sections. The ways in which Australia has sought to restrain the growth in health expenditures and the problems encountered in implementing these strategies are then discussed. The chapter concludes with a discussion of possible directions for reform to more effectively reduce incentives to oversupply health services and to improve the efficiency with which resources are used in the health-care sector.

Main features of the system

Structure of funding: an overview

The Australian health-care system blends both public and private arrangements for funding as well as the provision of medical services. Around 68 per cent (based on 1990 figures) of total health expenditures are public (Table 13). This is below the OECD average (77 per cent), but the difference has narrowed significantly over the past decade: most other OECD countries were reducing their public share while Australia was increasing its public share over this period.

Table 13.   **The public share in total expenditure on health**

Per cent

	1960	1970	1975	1980	1985	1990
Australia	**47.6**	**56.7**	**72.8**	**62.9**	**71.5**	**68.1**
Austria	69.4	63.0	69.6	68.8	66.7	66.1
Belgium	61.6	87.0	79.6	83.4	81.8	88.9
Canada	42.7	70.2	76.4	74.7	74.7	73.1
Denmark	88.7	86.3	91.9	85.2	84.4	83.6
Finland	54.1	73.8	78.6	79.0	78.6	80.9
France	57.8	74.7	77.2	78.8	76.9	74.5
Germany	66.1	69.6	77.2	75.0	73.6	71.8
Greece	64.2	53.4	60.2	82.2	81.0	84.2
Iceland	76.7	81.7	87.2	88.2	87.0	86.8
Ireland	76.0	81.7	79.0	82.2	77.4	74.7
Italy	83.1	86.4	86.1	81.1	77.1	77.8
Japan	60.4	69.8	72.0	70.8	72.7	70.8
Luxembourg			91.8	92.8	89.2	91.4
Netherlands	33.3	84.3	73.4	74.7	75.1	71.5
New Zealand	80.6	80.3	83.9	83.6	86.3	82.2
Norway	77.8	91.6	96.2	98.4	96.5	94.5
Portugal		59.0	58.9	64.3	54.6	54.6
Spain	58.7	65.4	77.4	79.9	80.9	80.5
Sweden	72.6	86.0	90.2	92.5	90.3	89.7
Switzerland	61.3	63.9	68.9	67.5	66.1	68.4
Turkey		37.3	49.0	27.3	50.2	35.6
United Kingdom	85.2	87.0	91.1	89.4	85.8	84.1
United States	24.5	37.3	41.6	41.9	40.3	41.1
European Community (12)[1]	67.5	77.5	79.3	81.2	79.4	79.2
OECD[1,2]	63.9	73.8	77.6	78.1	77.4	76.8

1.   Arithmetic average excluding Luxembourg and Portugal.
2.   Also excludes Turkey.
Source: OECD, *OECD Health Systems.*

Public health expenditures are financed from general taxation, supplemented by the (Commonwealth) income-related Medicare tax. The Medicare levy finances around 8 per cent of total health expenditure and 17 per cent of Commonwealth health outlays. Around 44 per cent of total health expenditure is derived from Commonwealth revenue sources and 23 per cent from States' own revenue sources (including Commonwealth Financial Assistance Grants to States).[74]

An estimated 60 per cent of public expenditure is used to subsidise access to private-sector providers in the areas of: community-based medical care; hospital-based medical care; pharmaceutical products; allied health care by optometrists and dentists; domiciliary care; and long-term care for the aged. The remaining 40 per cent of public expenditure mainly finances Medicare-designated (*i.e.* public) hospitals (most of which are publicly-owned hospitals) which provide core hospital infrastructure and teaching functions.[75]

Private sources account for 32 per cent of total health expenditure and include both patient out-of-pocket costs and payments from private insurance. Patient out-of-pocket expenses account for around two-thirds of these expenditures and private insurance premiums for most of the rest. Around 16 per cent of private expenditure pays for access to public-sector providers (mainly accommodation and other charges for private patients in public hospitals).

In practice, the Commonwealth government has a leadership role in health policy making. Until recently it had a role in direct provision of health care to war service veterans. The Commonwealth is now, however, in the final stages of either selling its hospitals to the private sector or transferring them to State health authorities. In future it will act as a purchaser of these services. State governments have responsibility for the planning, provision and administration of publicly owned and operated health-care services – hospitals, community health clinics and domiciliary care services. The majority of acute-care beds are in the publicly-owned hospital system and the majority of State health funding is channelled into this system.

Financing arrangements

Medicare

Australia has a compulsory, national funding scheme known as Medicare, which is run by the Commonwealth government. This scheme, introduced in 1984, aims to provide all Australian residents with: access to essential health-care services, with priority according to clinical need; quality health care, taking account of appropriateness of care and efficiency of delivery; and affordability of health care, both for the nation and for the individual. This scheme subsidises access to privately rendered medical services (Medical Benefits) and to prescription drugs dispensed in the community (Pharmaceutical Benefits). It also provides capped grants to States towards the costs of running Medicare-designated (*i.e.* public) hospitals, which agree in return to treat public patients free of charge.

The privately rendered medical services for which Medicare pays rebates include those in both the ambulatory (*i.e.* non-inpatient) sector and the inpatient sector for private patients. Private patients have free choice of doctor for such services; in contrast, inpatients opting for public-patient status do not have free choice of doctor. Medicare does not pay rebates for most allied health services (*e.g.* dental treatment and physiotherapy) for the general public but does ensure that these services are available to the socially disadvantaged free of charge or at little out of pocket cost.

The schedule of fees upon which Medical rebates are based is known as the Medical Benefits Schedule (MBS). Annual adjustments to Schedule fees have been unilaterally fixed by the government since the mid-1980s. For ambulatory services, the reimbursement by Medicare is 85 per cent of the Schedule fee plus a top-up if out-of-pocket expenses (*i.e.* the difference between the Medicare rebate and the Schedule fee) exceed an indexed limit either for a family group or an individual.[76] To the extent that charges exceed the Schedule fee, the excess must be borne by the patient (private gap insurance is not permitted). In the case of inpatient medical services received as a private patient, the Medicare rebate is 75 per cent of the Schedule fee with no limit on individual out-of-pocket expenses; private insurance may cover the gap between the Medicare rebate and the Schedule fee, but not the excess of fees charged above the Schedule fee. Although medical practitioners are free to set whatever fees they like, rates of compliance with the Schedule are generally high.[77] Persons electing to be treated as private inpatients in a hospital are responsible for both the hospital charges and doctors' fees, subject to any reimbursement *via* private health insurance or Medicare respectively. Medicare does not cover such items as theatre fees, recovery ward charges, drugs, dressings, etc., however, these may be covered under private insurance.

With respect to Pharmaceutical Benefits, the subsidies are based on the Pharmaceutical Benefits Schedule (PBS), which lists prices for all eligible prescription drugs. These prices are fixed through negotiations between a government body (the Pharmaceutical Benefits Pricing Authority) and drug companies. Patients pay only the first A$ 16.20 for their PBS drugs until total family expenditure on drugs reaches A$ 407.60 in a year. Thereafter, the co-payment is reduced to A$ 2.60 for all further drugs that year. For concessional patients (means-tested beneficiaries), the co-payment is A$ 2.60 for their first 52 prescriptions (again on a family basis) per year, after which there is no co-payment; hence the maximum out-of-pocket expenditure for concessional patients is A$ 135.20 per family per year. All of these amounts are indexed.

The introduction of Medicare reduced the cost of medical care to consumers by cutting the extent of cost sharing. The part of medical bills normally paid by public insurance in Australia rose from an estimated 62.2 per cent in 1980 to 70 per cent in 1990 (Table 14). As there was already universal public health insurance in 1980, this increase was largely due to a rise in the overall public co-payment for medical care.[78] Almost all other OECD countries also have universal public-health insurance but the public-insurance contribution to medical bills is generally higher than in Australia. The overall public co-payment in OECD countries is typically estimated to have been between 80 and 85 per cent in 1990, largely unchanged from a decade earlier. This trend masks the increasing concentration of expenditures on the chronically ill, who tend to have zero co-payments, and rising co-payments for other patients.

Private insurance

Voluntary private health insurance can be purchased to supplement Medicare for hospital care and for allied health care not covered by Medicare; private insurance is not permitted for ambulatory health care covered by Medicare. Private hospital insurance covers treatment received as a private patient in either a public or a private hospital. The advantages for which private patients pay are quicker access to elective surgery in private hospitals, the freedom as inpatients to choose their doctor and access to more comfortable hospital accommodation. Such insurance may cover the gap between the MBS fee and the Medicare rebate (75 per cent of the schedule fee) as well as hospital accommodation charges. All other charges for private inpatients must be paid by the patient. Private insurers

Table 14. **Coverage by insurance programmes and public share of medical care billing**

	1960			1970			1980			1990		
	A	B	C	A	B	C	A	B	C	A	B	C
United States [1]	..	..	50.8	..	..	65.6	..	..	76.2	..	..	79.6
Japan	88.0	70.0	61.6	100.0	80.7	80.7	100.0	88.7	88.7	100.0	87.0	87.0
Germany	85.0	90.0	76.5	88.0	92.0	81.0	91.0	95.0	86.5	92.2	92.0	84.8
France	76.3	61.0	46.5	95.7	70.0	67.0	99.3	75.0	74.5	99.5	75.1	74.7
Italy	87.0	80.0	69.6	93.0	80.0	74.4	100.0	81.2	81.2	100.0	75.9	75.9
United Kingdom	100.0	93.0	93.0	100.0	93.0	93.0	100.0	93.0	93.0	100.0	93.0	93.0
Canada	68.0	52.1	35.4	100.0	75.0	75.0	100.0	86.2	86.2	100.0	82.0	82.0
Australia	**77.0**	**50.0**	**38.5**	**79.0**	**50.0**	**39.5**	**100.0**	**62.2**	**62.2**	**100.0**	**70.0**	**70.0**
Austria	78.0	85.0	66.3	91.0	85.0	77.4	99.0	84.0	83.2	99.0	84.0	83.2
Belgium	58.0	72.0	41.8	85.0	75.0	63.8	99.0	88.0	87.1	98.0	87.0	85.3
Denmark	95.0	80.0	76.0	100.0	85.0	85.0	100.0	85.0	85.0	100.0	85.0	85.0
Finland	55.0	57.5	31.6	100.0	78.3	78.3	100.0	83.7	83.7	100.0	82.0	82.0
Greece	30.0	70.0	21.0	55.0	70.0	38.5	88.0	80.0	70.4	100.0	85.0	85.0
Iceland	100.0	80.0	80.0	100.0	85.0	85.0	100.0	93.0	93.0	100.0	93.0	93.0
Ireland	85.0	75.0	63.8	85.0	80.0	68.0	100.0	93.0	93.0	100.0	90.0	90.0
Luxembourg	90.0	..	..	100.0	..	..	100.0	91.0	91.0	100.0	91.0	91.0
Netherlands	71.0	57.0	40.5	86.0	75.0	64.5	74.6	75.3	56.2	69.2	71.4	49.4
Norway	100.0	80.0	80.0	100.0	80.0	80.0	100.0	90.0	90.0	100.0	90.0	90.0
Portugal	18.0	..	..	40.0	..	..	100.0	..	..	100.0	..	..
Spain	54.0	70.0	37.8	61.0	70.0	42.7	83.0	90.0	74.7	99.0	90.0	89.1
Sweden	100.0	80.0	80.0	100.0	92.0	92.0	100.0	95.8	95.8	100.0	94.0	94.0
Switzerland	74.0	85.0	62.9	89.0	..	..	96.5	91.9	88.7	99.5	91.0	90.5
Turkey	5.8	..	..	26.9	..	..	38.4	..	..	55.1	..	..
New Zealand	100.0	..	..	100.0	..	..	100.0	..	..	100.0	..	..
OECD [2]	..	..	57.7	..	..	71.1	..	..	82.9	..	..	83.5

A = Coverage of public insurance schemes as a percent of total population.
B = Part of medical bills normally paid for by public insurance schemes.
C = (A × B)/100.
1. Value for the United States represents the share of total health spending covered by public and private insurers.
2. Arithmetic average.
Source: OECD, *OECD Health Systems.*

are able to offer cover for ancillary services with few regulatory impediments. Premiums for private insurance must be set on the basis of community-risk rating rather than an assessment of individuals' medical risk. This is underwritten by risk-pooling arrangements whereby costs for high service users are spread amongst the insurers. In 1994, around 37 per cent of Australians bought private insurance for hospital cover and 36 per cent purchased allied health cover. These levels were much lower than a decade ago, when around 50 per cent of Australians purchased private health insurance. The out-of-pocket costs for health care for someone with comprehensive private health insurance are compared with those for someone without such insurance in Box 3.

Providers and how they are paid

As in the majority of other OECD countries, general practitioners (GPs) are mostly self-employed and charge a fee for service (Table 15); the few exceptions tend to work in community clinics, Aboriginal health services or women's clinics. Access to specialists is by referral from GPs, who therefore play a gatekeeping role to the rest of the system; this is also the case in most other OECD countries (see Table 15). Specialists in public hospitals are paid in one of two ways: as staff specialists who are employees of the hospital and are paid a salary; or as Visiting Medical Officers (VMOs), independent practitioners who are paid a fee on a sessional- or a per-service basis under contracts with the

---

Box 3. **Out-of-pocket costs with and without private health insurance**

	With private insurance	Without private insurance
Hospital care		
Public patient	Zero.	
Private patient	All expenses except MBS and accommodation charges.	All expenses except 75 per cent of MBS.
Ambulatory care.		
Medical (*e.g.* GP consultation)	Excess of fees over 85 per cent of MBS.	
Allied health care (*e.g.* dentistry)	Little or nothing for means-tested beneficiaries otherwise, depends on insurance policy.	Little or nothing for means-tested beneficiaries otherwise, all expenses.
Pharmaceuticals		
Public or private patient in public hospital	Nothing.	
Private patient in private hospital	Insurance generally covers pharmaceuticals.	All expenses.
Community pharmacy	First A$ 16.20 until family's annual expenditure totals A$ 407.60, then A$ 2.60. Means-tested beneficiaries pay A$ 2.60 for the first 52 prescriptions, then free.	

Table 15. **Arrangements for paying doctors and for access to specialists**

	Fee for service [1]	Capitation [2]	Wage and salary [3]	GP [4] gatekeeper
Australia	X			X
Austria	X			X
Belgium	X			
Canada	X			X
Denmark		X		X
Finland			X	
France	X			
Germany	X			X
Greece	X			
Iceland		X		X
Ireland		X		X
Italy		X		X
Japan	X			
Luxembourg	X			
Netherlands		X		X
New Zealand	X			X
Norway	X			X
Portugal			X	X
Spain [5]		X		X
Sweden			X	
Switzerland	X			
United Kingdom		X		X
United States	X			

1. Doctors are paid on the basis of services provided.
2. Doctors are paid a fee for a certain period for each patient registered with them, and this covers all primary care received.
3. Doctors are employed by the state or insurer to serve the insured population.
4. A referral from a primary physician is required for a consultation with a specialist.
5. Capitation up to 1983 and subsequently switching slowly towards wages and salaries.
Source: Gerdtham *et al.* (1995).

hospitals. Both categories of specialists retain the right of private practice. Many specialists combine private practice (including treating private patients in public hospitals) with VMO work in public hospitals. Specialists in private practice set their own fees.

The extensive use of fee-for-service arrangements for paying doctors combined with universal insurance tends to encourage oversupply of services. This incentive is intensified by the limited scope most doctors have to increase their incomes by raising prices. For some GPs and many specialists, the main constraints to higher prices are that the government unilaterally sets the MBS, generally relating increases to Accord wage increases, and that gap insurance is banned for ambulatory medical services and for that part of inpatient fees above the MBS. For most GPs, however, the binding constraint is their large and growing number.

The freedom to combine private practice with work in public hospitals enjoyed by specialists is an incentive to allocate as little of their time as possible to elective surgery for public patients as this is less well paid than private practice (non-elective surgery is mostly carried out on a public patient basis). The extent to which this can be done is increased by the possibility of treating inpatients privately in public hospitals. This makes possible private treatment for conditions requiring specialised infrastructure which may not be available in private hospitals or, if it is available, would incur higher user charges. Specialists nevertheless have an incentive to allocate some of their time to elective surgery for public patients, as this "buys" access to public infrastructure to treat private patients. These incentives contributed to long waiting lists for public patients to receive certain elective surgery (see below), especially in fields in which there is a shortage of specialists and/or there is little need for access to public hospital infrastructure for carrying out the treatment.

The (acute-care) hospital sector comprises both public and private hospitals. Public hospitals are mainly owned and operated by State governments. There are also some not-for-profit hospitals which are designated as public hospitals and government funded, though privately owned (mainly by religious organisations). Around 22 per cent of admissions to public hospitals are private patients. Private hospitals, in the past, tended to be mostly not-for-profit. However, in recent times for-profit organisations have entered the private hospital market and are expected to gain control of a significant number of private hospitals over the next few years. At the end of January 1995, there were 325 private hospitals in Australia compared with around 700 public hospitals. Less than 25 per cent of all acute-care beds are in private hospitals, and a similar proportion of all inpatients are treated there. Most private hospitals are small and do not provide a comprehensive range of services, although more complex procedures are increasingly being offered. Private hospitals tend not to operate accident and emergency departments nor to employ full time medical staff. In contrast, in the long-term care sector private nursing homes provide 84 per cent of beds.

One interesting feature in the delivery of hospital care has been the development of day hospitals or day surgeries. These are licensed private hospitals without overnight beds. In 1987 there were 9 such facilities. However, this has grown to 117 as at February 1995; a reflection on the increased awareness of the benefits of day surgery as a cost effective alternative to overnight stays in hospital. These day hospital facilities are all for-profit and many are owned by medical practitioners.

Public hospitals receive capped budgets from State governments, usually determined on the basis of historic allocations, but increasingly on the basis of prospective casemix, *i.e.* average costs of treatment times the projected number and mix of treatment (see below for a more detailed description). Capital funds for public hospitals (representing some 7 per cent of public health expenditure) are provided from a separate state vote and are costless for hospitals. Private hospitals presently charge on a fee-for-service basis but under pressure from private insurance funds will increasingly be paid on the basis of casemix.

The budget limits on public hospitals encourage them to shift costs onto Medicare and the private sector. This is done by withdrawing from as much service as possible, forcing patients to seek treatment privately. The public hospital is then relieved of the cost of treating some public patients and, indeed, can earn additional revenue from accommodation charges for private patients in public hospitals. The costs of treating additional private patients are instead met by Medicare (through subsidies for private care and drugs), private insurance and individuals' out-of-pocket expenses. State governments have, at least until recently, had few effective incentives to dissuade public hospitals from embarking on such cost-shifting exercises. Thus, there has been a community of interest between specialists and public hospitals in shifting costs to Medicare and the private sector.

For public hospitals funded on the basis of historic costs, there are few incentives to manage resources efficiently – more throughput or better quality services are simply not rewarded. Moreover, hospital managers are encouraged to spend all the funds allocated to them before the end of the financial year, regardless of the quality of these expenditures, so as not to be penalised in the following year's funding allocation. Separate capital funding is also a barrier to efficient resource utilisation as it prevents hospital managers from substituting between capital and other inputs in order to increase productivity.

Health status and satisfaction with the system

Health status indicators

As in other OECD countries, Australian health outcomes have improved considerably in the past few decades, and are generally a little better than the average for these countries. Life expectancy for a female born in Australia has increased from 74.0 in 1960 to 80.1 years in 1990, while for males the increase has been from 67.9 in 1960 to 73.9 in 1990 (Table 16). There have also been substantial increases in life expectancy for older adults, with life expectancy at age 60 rising from 19.5 years in 1960 to 23.2 years in 1990 for women and from 15.6 to 18.9 years for males. These latter increases are a marked improvement on developments in earlier decades: Australian Institute of Health and Welfare (AIHW) data show that life expectancy at age 65 increased by only 2.1 years for women and by 0.5 years for men between 1920-22 and 1960-62.[79]

Premature death,[80] defined as years of life lost before age 65 from avoidable causes, has been halved during the past three decades (Table 17). Australia's gains in avoiding premature death have been smaller than in most other OECD countries, largely reflecting Australia's better starting position. Potential years of female life lost in Australia are now slightly above the OECD average while potential male years of life lost remain below average. As in other OECD countries, a major factor underlying the reduction in premature deaths in Australia during the past three decades has been the substantial drop since the late 1960s in the number of premature deaths from cardiovascular and respiratory diseases (Diagram 23). These gains have been made possible by substantial advances in medical technology, such as cardiovascular therapies, and by changes in life-style, particularly involving less smoking and a move to lower cholesterol diets. At the same time, Australia and most other OECD countries have experienced some smaller increases in potential years life lost from cancers, particularly breast cancer and lung cancer.

There have also been marked improvements in perinatal[81] and infant mortality[82] during the past three decades (Table 18). Australia's perinatal mortality rate has fallen from 2.9 per cent in 1960 to 0.6 per cent in 1990. This improvement was slightly larger than the OECD average, which fell from 3.1 per cent to 0.8 per cent. By contrast, the drop in Australia's infant mortality rate, from 2.0 per cent in 1960 to 0.8 per cent in 1990, was smaller than the OECD average,

Table 16. Life expectancy

	Female life expectancy						Male life expectancy					
	At birth		At 60		At 80		At birth		At 60		At 80	
	1960	1990	1960	1990	1960	1990	1960	1990	1960	1990	1960	1990
United States	73.1	78.8	19.5	22.8	6.8	9.0	66.6	71.8	15.8	18.5	6.0	7.1
Japan	70.2	81.9	17.8	24.4	5.9	8.7	65.5	75.9	14.8	20.0	4.9	6.9
Germany	72.4	79.1	18.5	22.2	5.9	7.7	66.9	72.7	15.5	17.8	5.2	6.1
France	73.6	80.9	19.5	24.2	6.3	..	67.0	72.7	15.6	19.0	5.1	..
Italy[1]	72.3	80.4	19.3	23.1	6.4	..	67.2	74.0	16.7	18.6	5.7	..
United Kingdom	74.2	78.5	19.3	21.8	..	8.2	68.3	73.0	15.3	17.5	..	6.2
Canada[1]	74.3	80.4	19.9	23.7	7.0	9.3	68.4	73.8	16.8	18.9	6.2	7.1
Australia	**74.0**	**80.1**	**19.5**	**23.2**	**..**	**8.7**	**67.9**	**73.9**	**15.6**	**18.9**	**..**	**6.9**
Austria	71.9	79.0	18.6	22.3	5.9	7.6	65.4	72.5	15.0	18.1	5.1	6.6
Belgium	73.5	79.1	18.7	22.5	..	7.9	67.7	72.4	15.4	17.8	..	6.1
Denmark	74.1	77.7	19.1	21.7	..	8.1	72.3	72.0	17.2	17.5	..	7.1
Finland	71.6	78.9	17.5	21.9	5.1	7.5	64.9	70.9	14.4	17.1	5.5	6.1
Greece	70.4	..	18.6	..	5.9	7.7	67.3	..	16.9	..	5.6	..
Iceland	75.0	80.3	20.4	23.3	7.1	9.0	70.7	75.7	18.6	20.0	6.2	7.4
Ireland	71.8	77.5	18.3	20.8	5.4	..	68.5	72.0	16.3	16.7	..	..
Luxembourg	71.9	78.5	18.3	22.4	5.4	..	66.1	..	15.9	17.8	5.0	..
Netherlands	75.5	80.1	19.9	22.7	..	8.0	71.6	73.8	17.8	17.7	..	6.2
New Zealand	73.9	78.3	19.5	22.2	..	8.4	68.7	72.4	16.3	18.2	..	6.8
Norway	75.9	79.8	20.1	..	..	8.1	71.4	73.4	18.0	..	..	6.4
Portugal	67.2	77.9	18.6	21.2	..	6.7	61.7	70.9	15.9	17.2	..	5.7
Spain	72.2	80.5	19.2	23.5	6.5	8.2	67.4	73.4	16.5	19.2	5.7	6.9
Sweden	74.9	80.4	19.3	23.3	6.2	8.3	71.2	74.8	17.3	19.1	5.7	6.6
Switzerland	74.1	80.9	19.2	23.9	6.1	8.5	68.7	74.0	16.2	19.1	5.5	6.8
OECD[2]	73.0	79.5	19.1	22.7	6.2	8.2	67.9	73.1	16.3	18.3	5.5	6.6

1. Data are for 1961.
2. Arithmetic average.
Source: OECD, OECD Health Systems.

Table 17. **Declining trends in premature death,**[1] **1960-90**

Years gained per 100 000, under 65 years of age

	Potential female years of life lost			Potential male years of life lost		
	1960	1990	Gain	1960	1990	Gain
United States	6 217.2	3 082.7	3 134.5	8 652.8	4 579.7	4 073.1
Japan	7 829.5	1 643.2	6 186.3	9 303.8	2 509.7	6 794.1
Germany	6 677.4	2 375.0	4 302.4	8 548.7	3 746.7	4 802.0
France	5 541.4	2 099.7	3 441.7	7 777.0	3 869.4	3 907.6
Italy	8 672.2	2 452.0	6 220.2	10 767.3	3 847.5	6 919.8
United Kingdom	5 279.8	2 688.4	2 591.4	7 323.3	3 614.0	3 709.3
Canada	5 770.0	2 283.9	3 486.1	7 628.6	3 117.7	4 510.9
Australia	**5 273.9**	**2 466.8**	**2 807.1**	**6 823.0**	**3 338.7**	**3 484.3**
Austria	7 016.6	2 356.4	4 660.2	9 210.4	3 392.4	5 818.0
Belgium	6 203.0	2 675.3	3 527.7	8 913.2	3 986.8	4 926.4
Denmark	4 801.4	2 714.5	2 085.9	5 740.0	3 643.3	2 096.7
Finland	5 255.5	1 943.9	3 311.6	7 886.4	2 679.6	5 206.8
Greece	7 642.9	2 417.2	5 225.7	9 021.7	3 666.7	5 355.0
Iceland	4 059.1	2 080.0	1 979.1	5 948.2	1 985.4	3 962.8
Ireland	7 143.2	2 715.4	4 427.8	8 723.9	3 709.1	5 014.8
Luxembourg	6 001.6	2 186.7	3 814.9	7 928.1	3 466.7	4 461.4
Netherlands	4 285.7	2 333.8	1 951.9	5 664.2	3 389.8	2 274.4
New Zealand	5 651.2	2 358.2	3 293.0	7 078.1	2 847.5	4 230.6
Norway	4 408.0	2 368.9	2 039.1	5 804.4	2 652.1	3 152.3
Portugal	14 963.7	3 277.1	11 686.6	18 354.0	5 500.6	12 853.4
Spain	7 901.6	2 449.6	5 452.0	9 883.0	4 037.5	5 845.5
Sweden	4 204.3	1 841.1	2 363.2	4 917.5	2 449.2	2 468.3
Switzerland	4 600.9	2 018.4	2 582.5	6 176.4	2 806.5	3 369.9
OECD[2]	6 321.7	2 383.9	3 937.9	8 177.1	3 427.7	4 749.5

1. Premature death from all causes less external causes (which include motor vehicle accidents) less suicides.
2. Arithmetic average.
Source: OECD, *OECD Health Systems.*

mainly reflecting Australia's more favourable starting position. Nevertheless, the infant mortality rate in Australia is now slightly above the OECD average.

The health status of the Aboriginal population has also been improving over the past two decades.[83] Higher life expectancy, reduced infant mortality and a lower burden of infectious and parasitic diseases are all evidence of improvement. However, as reflected in rates of hospitalisation, maternal mortality and disability, and in continuing high mortality in adults, the burden of disease for Aboriginals continues to be higher than in non-Aboriginal Australians (see

Diagram 23A. **POTENTIAL YEARS OF LIFE LOST**[1]

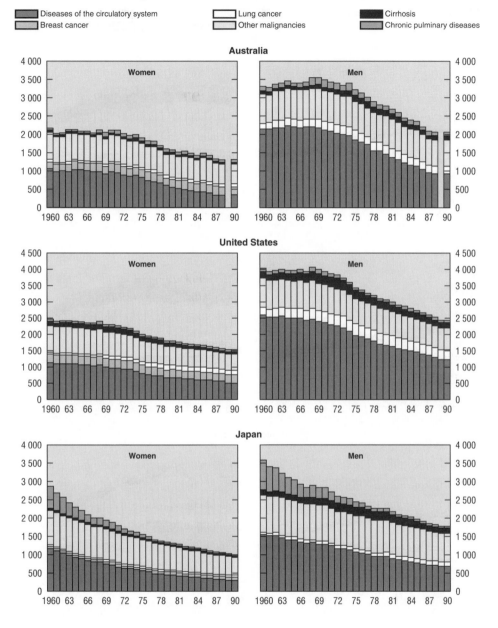

■ Diseases of the circulatory system   ☐ Lung cancer   ■ Cirrhosis
▨ Breast cancer   ▨ Other malignancies   ▨ Chronic pulminary diseases

Australia

Women — **Men**

United States

Women — **Men**

Japan

Women — **Men**

1.   Years lost per 100 000 equivalent population aged 0-64.
Source: OECD Health Systems.

Diagram 23B. POTENTIAL YEARS OF LIFE LOST[1]

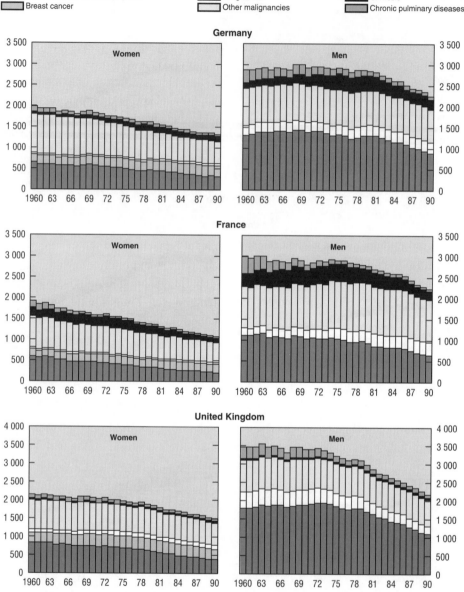

1. Years lost per 100 000 equivalent population aged 0-64.
Source: OECD Health Systems.

86

Table 18. **Perinatal and infant mortality** [1]

	Perinatal mortality		Infant mortality	
	1960	1990	1960	1990
United States	2.89	0.91	2.60	0.92
Japan	3.73	0.55	3.07	0.46
Germany	3.58	0.60	3.38	0.71
France	3.13	0.83	2.74	0.72
Italy	4.19	1.05	4.39	0.82
United Kingdom	3.36	0.81	2.25	0.79
Canada	2.84	0.77	2.73	0.68
Australia	**2.90**	**0.61**	**2.01**	**0.82**
Austria	3.50	0.69	3.75	0.78
Belgium	3.19	..	3.12	0.79
Denmark	2.62	0.83	2.15	0.75
Finland	2.75	0.62	2.10	0.56
Greece	2.64	1.19	4.01	0.97
Iceland	1.97	0.63	1.30	0.59
Ireland	3.77	1.02	2.93	0.82
Luxembourg	3.23	0.69	3.15	0.74
Netherlands	2.66	0.96	1.79	0.71
New Zealand	2.70	0.74	2.26	0.84
Norway	2.40	0.75	1.89	0.70
Portugal	4.11	1.26	7.75	1.10
Spain	3.66	0.76	4.37	0.76
Sweden	2.62	0.65	1.66	0.60
Switzerland	2.56	0.77	2.11	0.68
OECD [2]	3.09	0.80	2.94	0.75

1. Perinatal mortality is expressed as a percent of all births. Infant mortality is expressed as a percent of live births.
2. Arithmetic average.
Source: OECD, *OECD Health Systems.*

Annex I). This burden could be alleviated with an improvement in socio-economic factors such as unemployment and poor housing which influence Aboriginal health. Finding ways to deliver health services which better meet the special needs of Aboriginals could also help to improve health outcomes.

Satisfaction with the health system

Another indicator of the performance of the health system is the degree of community satisfaction with it. A recent poll[84] in eleven countries on community

Diagram 24. **SATISFACTION AS A FUNCTION OF HEALTH SPENDING**

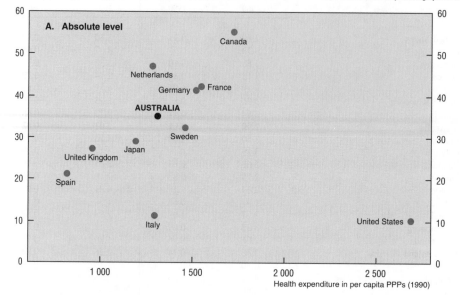

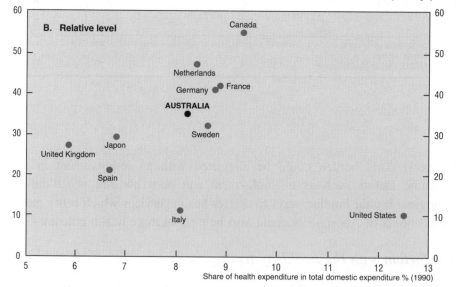

Source: Harvard Cuanter survey (in Blendon *et al.*, 1990) and *OECD Health Systems.*

88

satisfaction with the institutional health package available to them found that around 35 per cent of Australians were content with their system, an average level of satisfaction among the sample of countries (Diagram 24). Relating satisfaction to expenditure levels, the survey results suggest that there is only a weak relationship between expenditure levels and satisfaction (see Diagram 24). None of the other countries' health systems rates more highly than Australia's in terms of having a higher level of satisfaction for less expenditure but three countries' systems (the United States, Italy and Sweden) rate lower.[85]

Community satisfaction with Medicare, the compulsory public insurance scheme, is high and rising. Independent market research shows that the proportion of the population rating Medicare highly increased from 46 per cent in 1987 to 54 per cent in 1993 and that in 1993 only 18 per cent of the population rated satisfaction with it as "fairly low" or "very low".[86] This research also finds a strong correlation between attitudes to Medicare and private health insurance status, with 65 per cent of respondents without private health insurance rating Medicare highly compared with only 39 per cent of persons with private insurance. And membership in private health insurance is falling sharply, having declined from 50 per cent of the population in 1984 to 39 per cent in 1993. The major reasons for dissatisfaction with Medicare appear to be hospital waiting lists and poor hospital service, with 23 per cent of those surveyed in 1993 mentioning these factors.

Expenditure trends

Expenditure levels

As in other OECD countries, health-care expenditure is increasing as a share of GDP in Australia, having risen from 4.9 per cent in 1960 to 8.5 per cent in 1993 (Table 19). This share is slightly above the average for OECD countries but is nevertheless within the 7 to 9 per cent band into which most OECD countries fall; the major outliers from this band are the United States, at 14.1 per cent of GDP, and Turkey, at 3.9 per cent.

Table 19. **Total health expenditure as a percentage of GDP**

	1960	1970	1975	1980	1985	1990	1992	1993
United States	5.3	7.3	8.4	9.3	10.8	12.7	13.8	14.1
Japan	3.0	4.6	5.6	6.6	6.6	6.8	7.0	7.3
Germany	4.8	5.9	8.1	8.4	8.7	8.3	8.6	8.6
France	4.2	5.8	7.0	7.6	8.5	8.9	9.4	9.8
Italy	3.6	5.2	6.1	6.9	7.0	8.1	8.6	8.5
United Kingdom	3.9	4.5	5.5	5.6	5.9	6.0	7.0	7.1
Canada	5.5	7.1	7.2	7.4	8.5	9.4	10.2	10.2
Total of above countries	4.3	5.8	6.8	7.4	8.0	8.6	9.2	9.4
Australia	**4.9**	**5.7**	**7.4**	**7.3**	**7.7**	**8.2**	**8.5**	**8.5**
Austria	4.4	5.4	7.3	7.9	8.1	8.4	8.9	9.2
Belgium	3.4	4.1	5.9	6.6	7.4	7.6	8.1	8.1
Denmark	3.6	6.1	6.5	6.8	6.3	6.3	6.6	6.7
Finland	3.9	5.7	6.4	6.5	7.3	8.0	9.4	10.1
Greece	2.9	4.0	4.1	4.3	4.9	5.3	5.5	5.7
Iceland	3.3	5.0	5.8	6.2	7.3	7.9	8.9	8.3
Ireland	3.8	5.3	7.6	8.7	7.8	6.7	6.8	6.7
Luxembourg	..	3.8	5.2	6.3	6.2	6.0	5.9	5.9
Netherlands	3.8	5.9	7.4	7.9	7.9	8.0	8.5	8.7
New Zealand	4.3	5.2	6.7	7.2	6.4	7.4	7.7	7.7
Norway	3.3	5.0	6.7	6.6	6.4	7.5	8.3	8.2
Portugal	..	2.8	5.6	5.8	6.3	6.6	7.1	7.3
Spain	1.5	3.7	4.9	5.7	5.7	6.6	6.9	7.0
Sweden	4.7	7.1	7.9	9.4	8.9	8.6	7.9	8.0
Switzerland	3.3	5.2	7.0	7.3	8.1	8.4	9.4	9.9
Turkey	..	2.5	2.7	3.3	2.2	2.9	2.9	2.7
European Community (12)[1]	3.6	4.7	6.2	6.7	6.9	7.0	7.4	7.5
OECD [1,2]	3.9	5.2	6.6	7.1	7.3	7.7	8.2	8.3

1. Arithmetic average.
2. Excludes Turkey.
Source: OECD, *OECD Health Systems.*

Health-care expenditure per capita in Australia converted to a common currency at purchasing power parities (PPPs) for GDP was around the OECD average in 1992, as was the case in many other countries (Diagram 25). Per capita health expenditure and income (both converted to US dollars at PPP exchange rates) tend to be highly correlated across countries (Diagram 26). In this regard, Australian per capita health expenditure is in line with what would be expected on the basis of the country's per capita income level.

Diagram 25. **HEALTH EXPENDITURE PER CAPITA IN (GDP) PPPs**[1]
1992, OECD = 100

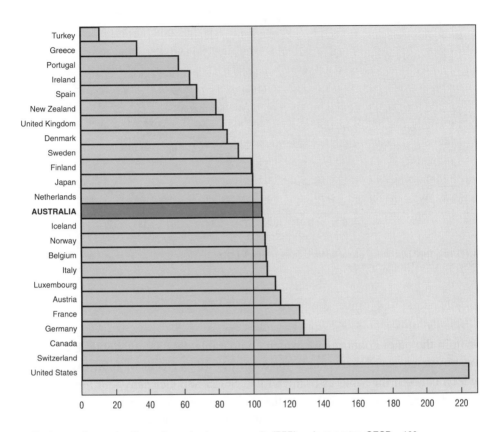

1.   Total expenditure on health care in purchasing power parity (PPP) exchange rates, OECD = 100.
Source: OECD Health Systems.

Allocation of expenditures

The allocation of health-care expenditures across sectors in Australia is similar to that in the United States (Diagram 27).[87] The inpatient sector, which mainly consists of (acute-care) hospitals and nursing homes, accounts for about half of health-care expenditures. This is about the same as in Canada, but higher

Diagram 26. **HEALTH EXPENDITURE AND GDP, 1992**

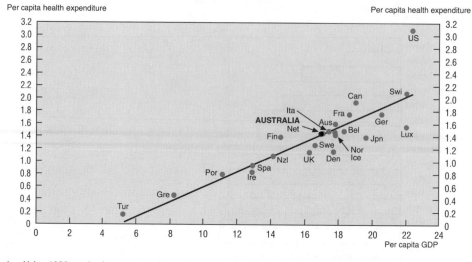

Per capita health expenditure

Per capita health expenditure

1. Using 1992 purchasing-power-parity exchange rates for GDP.
Source: OECD Health Systems.

than in the other countries for which comparable data are available. Expenditure on physician services accounts for a further 18 per cent of total expenditures, which is about the same as in the United States and Germany, but higher than in Canada and France and lower than in Japan.[88] Australian expenditures on pharmaceuticals represent 9 per cent of total expenditures, in line with the United States but much lower than in the other countries.[89]

Expenditure growth

Growth in real health expenditure per capita in Australia was 2.4 per cent over 1980-92, the same as the OECD average (Table 20). This growth rate was the same as in the United States, but lower than in the other G7 countries except Germany and the United Kingdom. The other important component of expenditure growth, medical-specific inflation,[90] averaged only –0.2 per cent in Australia over 1980-92, well below the OECD average of 0.6 per cent. While comparisons of price-volume splits of total spending on health across countries need to be treated with caution, it seems likely that spending restraint – to the extent that it

Diagram 27. **THE ALLOCATION OF HEALTH-CARE EXPENDITURES**
Selected OECD countries

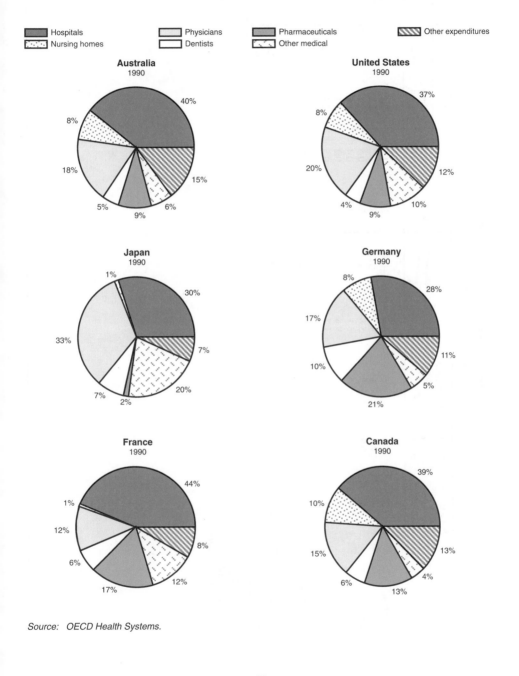

Source: *OECD Health Systems.*

Table 20. **Decomposition of health expenditure growth**

Average annual rates, 1980-92

	Share of total expenditure on health in GDP 1980	Nominal health expenditure growth	Health price deflator growth	GDP price deflator	Medical[1] specific price increases	Health care		Per capita		Share of total expenditure on health in GDP 1992
						Volume growth	Population growth	Volume growth	Real GDP growth	
Australia	**7.3**	**10.6**	**6.5**	**6.6**	**-0.1**	**3.9**	**1.5**	**2.4**	**1.0**	**8.5**
Canada	7.4	9.8	5.8	4.5	1.3	3.8	1.2	2.5	1.1	10.2
France	7.6	9.9	4.7	5.8	-1.0	5.0	0.5	4.4	1.5	9.4
Germany	8.4	5.8	3.5	3.1	0.3	2.2	0.4	1.8	1.9	8.6
Italy	6.9	14.0	10.4	9.8	0.6	3.3	0.2	3.1	1.8	8.6
Japan	6.6	6.2	2.2	1.7	0.5	3.9	0.5	3.4	3.3	7.0
United Kingdom	5.6	10.2	7.7	6.1	1.5	2.4	0.2	2.1	1.8	7.0
United States	9.3	10.4	6.8	4.3	2.4	3.4	1.0	2.4	1.4	13.8
European Community (12)[2]	6.7	11.1	8.0	7.6	0.3	2.9	0.3	2.6	2.0	7.4
OECD[2,3]	7.1	11.3	8.1	7.5	0.6	2.9	0.5	2.3	1.7	8.2

1. Medical specific inflation is defined as the excess of health care price increases over those on all goods and services.
2. Arithmetic averages.
3. Excludes Turkey.
Source: OECD, OECD Health Systems.

has occurred – has reflected the greater influence government has over medical inflation than expenditure volumes. As noted above, the government unilaterally fixes the MBS, which has been linked to Accord wage increases since the mid-1980s, and has considerable monopsony power in negotiations with drug companies over the PBS. In contrast, the government has little control over expenditure volumes on medical services and pharmaceutical goods, which are largely demand determined.

As a share of GDP, health expenditure rose by 1.2 percentage points over 1980-92, about the same as the average increase for OECD countries (see Table 20). This outcome, despite average growth in per capita expenditure volumes combined with low medical-specific inflation, reflects below average growth in per capita real GDP.

Factors underlying health expenditure growth

A number of factors help to explain the rising demand for health care generally in OECD countries, and in Australia in particular. These include rising incomes, population ageing and increased access and insurance cover; population ageing has been the same in Australia as the average for the OECD (see Box 4) while the increase in per capita income has been lower but the increase in

---

Box 4. Effects on health spending of ageing population structures

Ageing population structures in OECD countries are increasing demand for health care. Persons aged over 65 are estimated on average to account for roughly four times as much spending on health care as the rest of the population, although there is considerable variation between countries (OECD, 1987). Using this ratio (and making no allowance for the effects of technological change on supply or for behavioural changes on the demand of this group relative to the average), Oxley and MacFarlan (1995) estimate that ageing population structures may have added around 0.2 per cent to annual growth in health spending during the 1980s and could add 0.3 per cent during the 1990s in both Australia and the OECD area generally (Table 21). This compares with real health spending growth of 4 per cent per annum in Australia and an OECD average growth rate of 3 per cent over 1980-92. The effects of ageing population structures are, however, set to become more important, with this factor estimated to add 0.6 per cent to the growth rate of real health expenditure in Australia over 2000-2020 and 0.4 per cent over 2020-2040. Most other OECD countries are likely to experience a smaller increase in health spending due to ageing over 2000-2020 but a similar increase thereafter.

Table 21. **Effects on health spending of changes in population structure**[1]

	1980-90	1990-2000	2000-20	2020-40
United States	0.26	0.12	0.48	0.46
Japan	0.69	1.03	0.77	0.18
Germany		0.38	0.60	0.51
France		0.38	0.47	0.48
Italy		0.69	0.51	0.68
United Kingdom	0.16	−0.02	0.25	0.30
Canada	0.33	0.51	0.70	0.45
Australia	**0.22**	**0.27**	**0.57**	**0.38**
Austria	−0.08			
Belgium	0.03	0.62	0.29	0.60
Denmark	0.35	−0.06	0.48	
Finland	−0.11	0.78	0.46	0.21
Greece		0.83	0.41	0.46
Iceland		0.25	0.38	
Ireland		0.08	0.37	0.50
Netherlands		0.22	0.70	0.59
New Zealand	−0.16	−0.28	0.62	0.23
Norway	0.34			
Portugal	0.29	0.15	0.65	0.30
Spain	0.52	0.56	0.23	0.88
Sweden	0.34	−0.38	0.34	
Switzerland	0.17	0.22	0.37	0.28
Turkey	−0.22			

1. Table shows possible effects on health spending in each period (expressed as an annual average percentage change) due to changes in the proportion of those aged over 65 to those under 65. The simulation assumes that average health spending on the 65+ age group is four times as much as on those under 65.
Source: Oxley and MacFarlan (1995).

insurance cover (see Table 14) greater. Oxley and MacFarlan (1995) calculate that these factors might explain from 25 to 60 per cent (depending on the income elasticity of health expenditure) of the total increase in health expenditure in OECD countries between 1960 and 1990. The remainder of the increase is likely to be attribu table mainly to supply factors. Probably the most important of these is improvements in technology, defined broadly to include techniques, drugs, equipment and procedures used in providing health care. Increases in the supply of medical personnel and in physical facilities are also likely to have been important factors underlying growth in health expenditures.

Measures to restrain health expenditure growth in Australia

The Australian government has largely sought to restrain the growth in health expenditures through "macroeconomic" or "top-down" controls. These approaches emphasise constraints on growth in total expenditures rather than on altering microeconomic incentives to improve the efficiency with which resources are utilised. The principal measures used in Australia to control spending have been tight limits on budgets for public hospitals, the use of monopsony power to achieve low medical-specific inflation and measures to control the dissemination of new technology. The choice of these measures has been conditioned by institutional arrangements for health care in Australia – the government has leverage over health budgets and medical-specific inflation, but little control over volumes of ambulatory services, private inpatient medical services and pharmaceutical goods dispensed in the community. While there have also been some microeconomic reforms, including the introduction in some States of a purchaser-provider split based on casemix funding for public hospitals,[91] these reforms have not yet been broad enough to affect cost control or resource allocation in health-care supply.

Top-down expenditure controls

Inpatient

The major source of restraint on health expenditure growth in Australia during the 1980s was the capped budgets for public hospitals. This held growth in real expenditure on public hospitals to 26 per cent between FY 1982/83 and FY 1991/92, compared with an increase in total real recurrent health expenditure of 45 per cent (Tables 22 and 23). Expenditure on public hospitals fell from 36.0 per cent of total recurrent health expenditure in FY 1982/83 to 31.3 per cent in FY 1991/92.[92] Given the size of this sector, the slow growth in expenditure made a substantial contribution to restraint in growth in overall health expenditure. Private hospitals did not share in this expenditure restraint. Real expenditure for private hospitals grew by 68 per cent between FY 1982/83 and FY 1991/92, increasing their share of total recurrent health expenditure from 5.7 per cent to 6.6 per cent.[93]

Steps were also taken to slow the growth of nursing homes, the fees for which are largely paid by the government. Bed numbers were frozen at the 1983

Table 22.   **Total recurrent expenditure in acute hospitals** [1]

	Current prices			Constant 1989/90 prices			
	Public	Private	Total acute	Public	Private	Total acute	Per cent of GDP
Fiscal years							
1982/83	4 519	716	5 235	7 003	1 110	8 112	2.95
1983/84	4 878	803	5 681	7 120	1 172	8 292	2.84
1984/85	5 297	869	6 166	7 278	1 194	8 472	2.76
1985/86	5 784	969	6 753	7 512	1 258	8 770	2.75
1986/87	6 593	1 127	7 720	7 804	1 334	9 138	2.80
1987/88	7 249	1 216	8 465	8 138	1 365	9 503	2.77
1988/89	8 100	1 335	9 435	8 554	1 410	9 963	2.77
1989/90	8 736	1 540	10 276	8 736	1 540	10 276	2.78
1990/91	9 242	1 821	11 063	8 734	1 720	10 454	2.84
1991/92	9 613	2 024	11 637	8 833	1 860	10 693	2.88

1.   Acute hospitals includes recognised public, private and repatriation hospitals.
Source: Australian Institute of Health and Welfare, Health Expenditure Database.

level and access was made subject to an assessment of need. At the same time, there has been a shift in the balance between nursing home and hostel places; the frail elderly who are still mobile have been redirected towards the less costly alternatives of supported accommodation (hostels) or, if they are not so frail, their

Table 23.   **Total recurrent expenditure in acute hospitals,** [1]
percentage of total recurrent health expenditure

Constant 1989/90 prices

	Per cent			Recurrent health expenditure A$ million
	Public hospitals	Private hospitals	All acute hospitals	
Fiscal years				
1982/83	36.0	5.7	41.7	19 439
1983/84	34.6	5.7	40.2	20 603
1984/85	34.2	5.6	39.8	21 271
1985/86	33.5	5.6	39.2	22 396
1986/87	33.2	5.7	38.9	23 490
1987/88	33.4	5.6	39.1	24 335
1988/89	33.2	5.5	38.6	25 796
1989/90	32.5	5.7	38.3	26 849
1990/91	31.8	6.3	38.1	27 425
1991/92	31.3	6.6	37.8	28 263

1.   Acute hospitals includes recognised public, private and repatriation hospitals.
Source: Australian Institute of Health and Welfare, Health Expenditure Database.

own homes, but with domiciliary support services (such as home nursing care and delivered meals). To make this switch possible, the government expanded funding for supported accommodation and, in 1985, rationalised and expanded domiciliary support services through the introduction of the Home and Community Care programme.[94] The result has been a large expansion in the hostel sector and in the numbers of elderly people remaining in their homes with domiciliary support services.

Medical-specific inflation

Another important plank in the "top-down" strategy to contain growth in health expenditure has been the vigorous exercise of Medicare's monopsony power to keep medical-specific inflation in the ambulatory and pharmaceutical sectors low. MBS fees have been set unilaterally by the government since the mid-1980s, when the Australian Medical Association withdrew from the independent Tribunal initially established to set fees; the government has since linked rises in the MBS to Accord wage increases. Despite the fact that the government lacks the constitutional power to enforce the MBS fees that it unilaterally sets, compliance has risen to high levels in the past few years, with just over 80 per cent of all services billed at or below the MBS in December 1993. This has undoubtedly been facilitated by the increasing numbers of doctors. Compliance tends to be greatest for GPs, where the increase in doctor supply has been most marked, and lowest for specialists in short supply; GPs bill on average 6 per cent under the MBS, reflecting the large number who bill directly to Medicare,[95] while obstetricians/gynaecologists and anaesthetists in full time practice bill on average at 20 per cent and 18 per cent, respectively, over the MBS (Deeble, 1991). Largely reflecting the low increase in the MBS, medical-specific inflation in the ambulatory sector was held to an annual average rate of just 0.4 per cent over 1980-90, about the same as in the EC but a little over half the average for OECD countries (Table 24).

Pharmaceutical price inflation has also been restrained through the use of the government's monopsony power in the negotiations between its representative [the Pharmaceutical Benefits Pricing Authority (PBPA)]and the drug companies to fix pharmaceutical prices. The PBPA has succeeded in restraining pharmaceutical-specific inflation to an annual average rate of −0.9 per cent over 1980-90, well below the OECD average of zero over this period (see

Table 24. **Trends in relative price inflation for health care, 1970-90**[1]

Annual average growth rates

	Total spending		Hospital spending		Ambulatory spending		Pharmaceutical spending	
	1970-80	1980-90	1970-80	1980-90	1970-80	1980-90	1970-80	1980-90
Australia	**0.7**	**−0.3**	**1.6**	**−0.3**	**0.3**	**0.4**	**−4.0**	**−0.9**
United States	0.4	2.2	0.9	1.7	0.5	2.7	−2.2	3.2
Japan	−0.6	0.7	−1.8	0.5	−1.8	0.5	−2.4	1.2
Germany	0.5	0.5	6.7	1.4	2.6	−0.2	−1.3	1.9
France	−1.0	−1.1	0.6	0.0	−0.9	−1.7	−5.1	−3.5
Italy	0.0	0.5	1.3	2.2	−3.4	4.0	−8.8	−4.3
United Kingdom[2]	−0.5	1.2	3.2	0.9	..	..	−1.7	−1.0
Canada	0.3	1.2	2.4	1.8	−2.2	1.1	−3.5	4.5
European Community[3]	0.5	0.3	2.7	1.3	1.1	0.5	−3.0	−0.4
OECD average[3, 4]	0.5	0.5	2.2	1.1	0.7	0.7	−3.0	0.0

1. Growth in deflators for health care relative to the GDP deflator.
2. Hospital spending is for England only.
3. Arithmetic average.
4. Excludes Turkey.
Source: OECD, *OECD Health Systems.*

Table 24). This factor has been reinforced in recent years by a number of reforms to reduce prices further. A minimum pricing schedule for the PBS was introduced in 1991, according to which the Medicare subsidy is based on the cheapest generic substitute or branded-equivalent available for the prescribed drug. Should a more expensive drug be prescribed, patients must pay the difference between the actual cost and the minimum price; they can, alternatively, get their pharmacist to contact the doctor about changing the prescription. Applications to have new drugs listed on the PBS since 1991 have had to demonstrate their cost-effectiveness; this is in addition to the pre-existing requirement to demonstrate their safety and efficacy. If a new drug is considered to have no significant clinical advantages over existing drugs, it will only be listed on the PBS (and therefore subsidised) if the manufacturer accepts a price no greater than that applying to existing drugs. Tailored packaging has also contributed to the containment of pharmaceutical costs.

Fee-for-service volumes

High growth in service volumes in the fee-for-service sectors has been a particular problem in Australia. The volume of ambulatory services per capita

Table 25. **Trends in health-care volumes per capita**[1]

Annual average growth rates

	Total		In-patient		Ambulatory		Pharmaceutical	
	1975-80	1980-90	1975-80	1980-90	1975-80	1980-90	1975-80	1980-90
United States	3.3	2.6	4.0	2.2	2.8	2.8	2.3	0.5
Japan	6.1	3.1	6.2	3.0	4.7	2.3	..	..
Germany	3.7	1.3	0.2	0.4	2.1	2.1	5.1	0.7
France	5.3	4.5	6.7	2.6	5.0	6.5	3.9	7.7
Italy	6.3	3.2	9.1	0.6	8.0	−0.1	15.6	11.4
United Kingdom[2]	1.8	1.8	0.6	0.1	..	..	3.9	5.4
Canada	2.2	2.8	0.7	1.5	3.9	2.8	4.7	3.8
Australia	**1.0**	**2.5**	**2.6**	**1.5**	**1.5**	**3.6**	**−1.7**	**4.6**
Austria	2.8	1.0	1.2	−0.1	1.1	3.0	6.8	2.7
Belgium	4.7	2.8	4.7	1.2	4.5	4.1	5.0	2.1
Denmark	5.5	1.0	3.2	0.4	3.0	1.5	5.4	0.4
Finland	3.2	3.1	3.5	2.7	1.7	2.4	3.4	2.1
Greece	3.3	4.2	2.9	..			1.5	2.9
Iceland	4.5	4.3	9.8	3.9			7.3	3.0
Ireland	5.0	−1.5					−4.2	0.4
Luxembourg	7.0	2.8					7.1	3.0
Netherlands	1.6	1.4	0.9	0.2	3.5	2.2	1.2	4.3
Norway	4.0	2.5	6.4	1.8	..	3.9	14.2	1.7
Spain	4.3	4.4			..	3.8	..	..
Sweden	3.2	1.4					2.0	5.6
Switzerland	0.9	3.0			2.7	2.3	5.0	−1.5
OECD[3]	3.8	2.5	4.4	1.7	3.4	2.9	4.7	3.2

1. Deflated by the relevant health price deflators.
2. In-patient care is for England only, and for the public sector exclusively.
3. Arithmetic average.
Source: OECD, OECD Health Systems.

grew by 3.6 per cent per annum over the 1980s, while that for pharmaceutical goods grew by 4.6 per cent per annum (Table 25). Both rates are higher than in most other OECD countries.

One of the factors considered to be pushing up service volumes and the number of pharmaceutical prescriptions being written is the rising number of doctors, especially GPs. The number of practising physicians per capita rose at an annual rate of 2.3 per cent during the 1980s, somewhat below the OECD-average increase of 2.8 per cent; this increased the doctor-patient ratio to 2.2 per thousand inhabitants in 1990, which is near the OECD average (Table 26). In order to slow the growth in doctor numbers, restrictions were placed on the registration of

Table 26. **Practising physicians per capita**

Annual per cent growth and levels

	1960-70	1970-80	1980-90	Levels 1990 [1]	Proportion of specialists
United States	1.1	2.5	1.6	2.3	50.9
Japan	0.6	1.6	2.6	1.6	–
Germany	1.4	3.3	3.1	3.1	32.7
France	2.8	4.6	2.9	2.7	48.5
Italy	4.0	4.4	2.4	1.5	–
United Kingdom	..	..	1.5	1.4	–
Canada	2.5	2.1	1.7	2.1	41.3
Australia	**1.7**	**3.7**	**2.3**	**2.2**	**34.4**
Austria	0.0	1.6	2.9	2.1	47.7
Belgium	1.9	4.1	3.2	3.2	40.4
Denmark	1.5	4.5	2.5	2.8	–
Finland	5.1	6.4	3.4	2.4	54.1
Greece	2.6	4.1	3.4	3.4	32.7
Iceland	2.0	4.1	2.9	2.8	–
Ireland	..	1.1	1.8	1.5	–
Luxembourg	1.1	4.2	1.7	2.0	61.1
Netherlands	1.1	4.3	2.8	2.5	29.2
Norway	1.5	3.6	4.7	3.1	–
Portugal	1.4	7.4	3.7	2.8	33.0
Spain	1.4	5.6	5.2	3.8	–
Sweden	3.3	5.3	2.7	2.9	62.2
Switzerland	0.6	5.1	2.2	2.9	32.6
Turkey	2.8	4.6	3.9	0.9	48.3
New Zealand	–0.1	3.7	2.0	1.9	30.8
OECD [2]	1.8	4.0	2.8	2.4	

1. Doctors per thousand inhabitants.
2. Arithmetic average.
Source: OECD, *OECD Health Systems.*

immigrant doctors. The number of countries from which doctors receive automatic accreditation has been drastically cut and a quota limit placed on the number of places available for the accreditation examination. Although there have not yet been any moves to reduce the number of doctors being trained in Australia, this issue is presently being discussed by the health authorities and the medical schools. In another move to slow growth in medical-service volumes, the government introduced licensing of pathology collection centres, with a phased reduction in the number of such centres.[96] This followed very rapid growth in pathology service volumes.

Controlling the pace of introduction of new technology

The flow of new medical technology is a significant source of upward pressure on health expenditures in Australia, as in other OECD countries. While it can also lead to lower costs, improved technology has tended on balance to raise health-care expenditures by increasing the capacity to treat both illness and disabling conditions: cataract operations, renal dialysis, organ transplants, coronary by-pass, hip and knee replacements and micro surgery have increased the range of conditions which can be treated while advances in anaesthetics have significantly reduced the risks of operating on older patients.[97] Moreover, new image technology (magnetic resonance, scanners and endoscopy) has improved the capacity for diagnosis.[98] Some examples of the impact of new technologies on health expenditures in Australia are discussed in Box 5. An important, but unresolved issue is whether the type of technological change is affected by payment incentives.[99] To the extent that insurers are willing to pay for all new treatments with little regard to cost and doctors are paid on a fee-for-service basis

---

Box 5. New technology and health expenditures in Australia

One of the fastest growing areas of technological change is in diagnostic imaging technology. Australians received some 9.1 million diagnostic imaging services funded through Medicare Medical Benefits (MBS) in FY 1992/93, equating to one test for every 1.9 people. These services accounted for 5 per cent of all MBS services and 13 per cent of all MBS expenditure. Most of the growth has been in the sophisticated and often expensive diagnostic imaging technologies such as computed tomography (CT), ultrasound and nuclear resonance imaging. Over the last nine years, the number of services per person has increased by 6 per cent per year and dollars spent has increased by about 12.5 per cent per annum. Australia's experience with this technology has not been unusual.

Another example of the impact of new technology on health expenditures relates to laparoscopic cholecystectomy (gall bladder removal), an application of minimally invasive surgery (MIS) procedures. A recent study indicated that in both Canada and Australia cholecystectomy rates were relatively constant for some years prior to the introduction of laparoscopic cholecystectomy but surgery rates increased significantly after the new procedure became available, by 17 per cent in Canada and 24 per cent in Australia. While the use of the MIS procedure led to a reduction in average length of stay, these savings have been largely offset by the increase in the number of procedures performed. This demonstrates the importance of appropriate incentives for doctors if the potential economies of new technology are to be realised.

to use them, technological change will be focused so as to increase incomes in the health sector, driving up health costs. In these circumstances, were there to be health-care reform in other countries, especially the United States, which diminished the importance of fee-for-service payment arrangements, this could alter the focus of technological change and reduce the growth in health-care costs throughout the OECD area.

The Australian authorities have sought to restrain technology-related expenditure growth by rationalising the spread of new technologies. The Australian Health Technology Advisory Committee was established under the auspices of the National Health and Medical Research Council to evaluate existing and emerging technologies and to make recommendations to governments, health providers and patients on the benefits and risks of new technologies. Another step taken was the creation of the National Funded Centres programme for high-cost and high-skill interventions, such as heart-lung transplantation. This programme rationalises the spread of highly specialised facilities across the nation, ensures concentration of skills to maintain standards and controls costs through capped grants from a national funding pool. All States participate in the programme and patients from all parts of Australia are accepted for treatment at the designated centres without charge to the patients or to the referring hospital.

The government has also introduced alternatives to fee for service for specified high-cost technologies. For example, the diffusion of magnetic resonance imaging (MRI) in Australia has been constrained through a national programme of capped grants instead of subsidies on a fee-for-service basis. The programme provides for designated sites at the ratio of one machine per million inhabitants and gives priority to applications with proven health benefits. Access to medical benefits has also been modified for bone densitometry, with subsidy limited to certain conditions where densitometry has proven health benefits.

Microeconomic reforms

Casemix funding

Some State governments have sought to improve the efficiency of their public hospitals by introducing a purchaser-provider split into funding, as has recently been done on a wider scale in the British and New Zealand health systems. To do this, it has been necessary to develop a measure for valuing output. This measure, which was originally developed in the United States in the 1980s and was largely adapted in Victoria to Australian circumstances, is known as Diagnostic Related Group (DRG) episodes of care.[100] Each treatment episode available in a hospital is classified to a DRG on the basis of its average expected cost of treatment. Hospitals then receive funding on the basis of the value of their prospective DRG-weighted output; this is also known as casemix funding.[101] Those hospitals which have lower costs than the DRG-weighted output payment get to keep their operating surpluses, while hospitals with higher costs will have less money available in the following year. Funding flows from high-cost hospitals to low-cost hospitals. These arrangements encourage hospital managers to increase productivity so as to generate surpluses, and thereby provide a cushion against adverse developments in the future, and to avoid future funding cuts or possible dismissal. They also terminate the incentives under the historic cost allocation arrangements for hospital managers to spend all of their budget allocations by the end of the financial year, regardless of the usefulness of some of these expenditures, so as to reduce the risk of future budget cuts.

Victoria was the first state to introduce casemix funding, doing so from 1 July 1993. Since that time, public hospitals in Victoria have had their variable costs financed on the basis of their expected DRG-weighted output; fixed costs, which comprise 65 per cent of budgets, continue to be financed on the basis of historic allocations. Failure to achieve the contracted output levels results in funding cut-backs in the following year. Additional funding has also been available through the additional throughput pool (A\$ 40 million in FY 1993/94) for hospitals exceeding their contracted output levels and reducing waiting lists. The initial results have been extremely encouraging. Despite a 5 per cent budget cut (which followed a 5 per cent cut the year before), DRG-weighted separations (discharges) increased by 6 per cent in FY 1993/94 and there was a major decline in waiting lists, especially for urgent surgery.[102] Neither overall readmission rates, nor unplanned readmission rates have increased. A further 9 per cent budget cut is scheduled for FY 1994/95 but hospital output targets have been raised by up to 2 per cent. The authorities also aim to make substantial progress in reducing waiting lists for semi-urgent surgery. Victorian public hospitals have reduced their costs from 10 per cent above the national average before casemix was introduced to perhaps a little below average. The success of casemix funding in

Victoria has encouraged other States to adopt it, with South Australia doing so from 1 July 1994 and Queensland following suit on 1 January 1995.

Recently announced government reforms to private health insurance arrangements should encourage private hospitals and insurers to negotiate contracts based on casemix information. These reforms are discussed further below.

Reforms to improve the value of private health insurance

The government recently announced a series for reforms intended to improve the value of private health insurance. Legislation to give effect to these reforms went before the Parliament in early 1995. The most important part of these reforms is the lifting of the requirement (under the National Health Act) that insurance funds deal equally with all doctors and hospitals. Instead, funds will be able to shop around, using their bargaining power to negotiate lower prices and/or better quality service with preferred providers. By negotiating such arrangements, funds should be able to offer better value insurance cover to clients prepared to restrict their choice of health-care providers to the designated preferred providers. The potential to offer better value insurance cover will be further enhanced, at the same time, by permitting funds to form agreements with doctors which enable the funds to offer private health insurance that covers the full cost of (inpatient) medical services, eliminating out-of-pocket expenses. To qualify for this exemption to the ban on gap insurance, the agreements must specify the total fee to be charged by the doctor. The advantage for doctors is that insurance payments are no longer restricted to the MBS, while for patients the advantage will be prior knowledge of the costs of hospital care.

Limiting fee-for-service payment arrangements

As noted above, the government has introduced alternatives for fee-for-service payment arrangements for specified high-cost technologies, such as MRI. The same has been done in some areas in which there had been rapid growth in service volumes. For example, episodic fees were introduced in pathology where multiple tests were performed concurrently. In obstetric services, where there has also been rapid growth in service volumes, payment arrangements were changed from fee for service to a global payment so as to reduce incentives for overservicing in ante-natal care.

Policing overservicing by doctors

Measures have also been taken to counter over servicing by existing doctors. Legislation has been introduced which allows a government-established body to monitor doctors' practices for patterns of inappropriate servicing. Panels of doctors will consider the servicing patterns of those doctors where there is concern and may make recommendations for punitive actions, such as withdrawal of Medicare provider privileges or fines based on the extent of overpayment due to inappropriate practices. This new mechanism is expected to improve significantly controls on service volumes.

Introduction of co-payments

A co-payment for out-of-hospital medical services was introduced under the Medical Benefits Scheme in 1991 for all patients except those entitled to concession cards (*i.e.* pensioners and welfare beneficiaries). There was widespread opposition to this co-payment, and it was withdrawn after only three months. In view of the short period during which it was in place, it is not possible to provide any objective assessment of its impact. Nevertheless, the concentration of healthcare expenditures in a small number of high cost episodes suggests that copayments would be unlikely to make a significant difference to the growth in total expenditures; at least in the United States, 5 per cent of the population accounts for 50 per cent of outlays for acute care.[103]

The present co-payment of A$ 2.60 per prescription for aged pensioners was only introduced in 1990 – previously they received prescription drugs free of charge.[104] The impact of this co-payment was to reduce the volume of drugs sold by about 15 per cent, but the effect varied between drug groups. For over-the-counter drugs, the drop was over 30 per cent, while for drugs used for acute conditions there was almost no effect. As might be expected, this reduction in the volume of drugs for the aged proved to be a one-off event, with growth having since returned to 5 per cent per annum, the long-term trend growth rate.

Problems encountered in restraining expenditure

Institutional arrangements for health care in Australia have considerably limited the government's scope for imposing expenditure restraint. The main options open to government were to cap budgets for public hospitals and to restrict price increases for medical services and pharmaceuticals goods. These options were forcefully exercised. But there was little control over the volume of medical services in the ambulatory sector, which are almost entirely paid for on a fee-for-service basis, and the volume of pharmaceutical goods consumed. The result has been that expenditure restraint in the 1980s was focused on the hospital sector – expenditure growth in the ambulatory and pharmaceutical sectors fully accounted for the increase in the share of health expenditure in GDP (Diagram 28).

This is clearly not a very efficient way to allocate resources to health care. Expenditure restraint has been effected where possible, but this was not necessa-

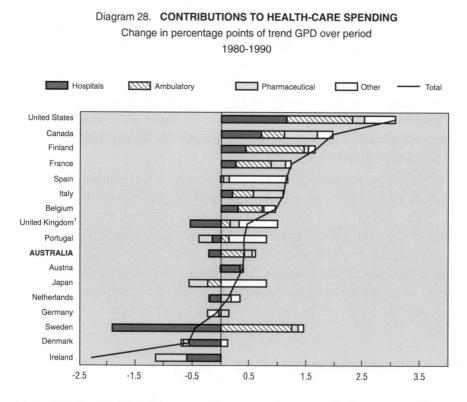

Diagram 28. **CONTRIBUTIONS TO HEALTH-CARE SPENDING**
Change in percentage points of trend GPD over period
1980-1990

1. Hospital data are for England only.
Source: OECD Health Systems.

rily where resources were being least efficiently used. And increasing amounts of resources were passively allocated to medical services and pharmaceutical goods. This problem was aggravated by the selective nature of Medicare subsidies, encouraging people to substitute wherever possible subsidised medical care for generally unsubsidised, but less costly, allied health care. Resources devoted to health care could have been more efficiently deployed had it been possible for government to plan rationally their allocation across health-care sectors and, indeed, to plan the total allocation of resources to health-care. Such planning is not possible so long as a large proportion of medical services is paid for on a fee-for-service basis and rigid demarcations persist in the way different segments of the health-care system are funded.

The demarcation in public funding between Medical Benefits (MB) and Pharmaceutical Benefits (PB) on the one hand, and public hospitals on the other, has encouraged hospitals to seek to alleviate the cap on funding by shifting costs onto the MB and PB schemes. This is done by withdrawing from as much medical care as possible in public hospitals, forcing patients to seek substitute care as private patients. The medical expenses incurred by those having chosen private-patient status are then subsidised by the MB scheme, regardless of whether the medical care is received in a hospital (including a public hospital) or a community setting. And to the extent that it is possible to dispense prescription drugs in a community setting, they are subsidised through the PB scheme. The rest of the health-care costs incurred by private patients for treatment received in the private sector are paid by private insurance and/or the patients themselves. With respect to treatment received in public hospitals, States also contribute by levying hospital charges which only cover about half of the costs incurred in treating private patients; of course, this is still less expensive for States than paying for all costs, as occurs for public patients.

This form of cost shifting has occurred through a variety of routes. Public hospitals have required pre-admission work-ups and post discharge follow-up to be done in doctors' private rooms rather than in hospital out-patient clinics. Patients have been given pharmaceutical starter packs (lasting only a few days) on discharge, with instructions to visit their GP for prescriptions for further treatments. Pathology laboratories within public hospitals have been privatised or corporatised. And out-patient arrangements have been manipulated so that doctors "bulk bill"[105] under the MBS, with Commonwealth benefits assigned by the doctor for payment direct to hospital trust accounts.

Some of these arrangements for cost shifting reduce the quality of patient care and result in inefficient service delivery. The moves to close or privatise hospital out-patient departments are eliminating the patterns of care which arose in this cost-constrained, but clinically rigorous, setting and replacing them with care having the characteristics of the uncapped Medicare fee-for-service sector.[106] As well, long established patterns of multi-disciplinary care for these patients are being eroded, as there is no equivalent in the MBS for physiotherapy, nutrition services, speech pathology and social work.[107] And the use of pharmaceutical starter packs increases the risk that discharged patients will not receive the combination of drugs intended by the specialist.

Another way in which patients may be encouraged to seek care privately instead of in public hospitals is to allow long public waiting lists for elective surgery to develop (Box 6); these do not, however, necessarily represent a

---

Box 6.   **Waiting lists for elective surgery**

Waiting lists for elective surgery constitute perhaps the major cause of public dissatisfaction with the Australian health care system. In the absence of comparable data, it is not possible to judge whether long waiting times for elective surgery is a more serious problem in Australia than in most other countries. Nevertheless, the following data suggest that there are grounds for public dissatisfaction. Based on data for large hospitals, there were an estimated 7.2 people per 1 000 waiting for elective surgery in 1994. The Australian Institute of Health and Welfare (AIHW) estimates an average clearance time[1] for the national waiting list to be 2.3 months. Data estimates from the AIHW's *National Report on Elective Surgery Waiting Lists for Public Hospitals 1994* show that 40 per cent of category 1[2] patients on waiting lists have waited over 30 days (Table 27). Patients waiting for elective surgery are likely to be waiting for cardio-thoracic (56 per cent of category 1 patients waiting over a month), orthopaedic (56 per cent), plastic (54 per cent) and ear, nose and throat surgery (44 per cent). The percentages of patients on waiting lists in these specialities who have waited over 12 months were 0 per cent, 8 per cent, 20 per cent and 11 per cent, respectively (Table 28).

---

1. Clearance time is defined as the number of patients waiting divided by the clearance rate.
2. Category 1 is defined as admission desirable within 30 days in the opinion of the treating clinician.

Table 27. Category 1[1] elective surgery patients[2]
Performance measures

	Clearance time[3] months	Patients waiting over 30 days at census date[4] per cent	Patients admitted after waiting over 30 days[5] per cent
Specialty			
Cardio-thoracic surgery	0.7	56	22
Ear nose and throat surgery	0.7	44	20
General surgery	0.5	34	11
Gynaecology	0.4	27	11
Neurosurgery	0.3	22	4
Opthalmology	0.9	43	14
Orthopaedic surgery	0.7	56	15
Plastic surgery	0.8	54	16
Urology	0.8	39	17
Vascular surgery	0.5	29	9
Other	0.2	33	7
All patients	0.6	40	13
Indicator procedure			
Cataract extraction	1.0	45	21
Cholecystectomy	1.1	48	21
Coronary artery bypass graft	1.0	66	43
Cystoscopy	1.0	40	21
Haemorrhoidectomy	0.7	49	12
Hysterectomy	0.9	36	20
Inguinal herniorrhaphy	0.8	49	19
Myringoplasty	1.1	57	18
Myringotomy	0.6	43	29
Prostatectomy	1.0	53	23
Septoplasty	1.1	59	44
Tonsillectomy	1.4	47	26
Total hip replacement	1.1	65	49
Total knee replacement	1.2	74	51
Varicose veins stripping and ligation	0.8	61	16

1. Category 1 patients are those for whom admission within 30 days is desirable in the opinion of the treating clinician. "Indicator procedures" comprise about one-quarter of the Category 1 waiting list census and about one-sixth of the Category 1 throughput.
2. The results are based on data from New South Wales, Victoria, Western Australia, Tasmania, the Australian Capital Territory and the Northern Territory. Australian Capital Territory data were not available for the calculations in column 3. Victorian data were not used for the calculations in columns 2 and 3 as they are not comparable with data from other States and Territories.
3. Calculated as (Category 1 patients on the waiting list at the census date)/[Category 1 patients cleared (admitted or removed) during the survey period] for each specialty or procedure.
4. Calculated as (Catetory 1 patients waiting >30 days at the census date)/(all Category 1 patients on waiting lists at the census date) for each specialty or procedure.
5. Calculated as (Category 1 patients admitted during survey period after waiting >30 days)/(all Category 1 patients admitted during the survey period) for each specialty or procedure.
Source: Australian Institute of Health and Welfare.

Table 28. **All elective surgery patients**[1]

Performance measures

	Clearance time[2] months	Patients waiting over 12 months at census date[3] per cent	Patients admitted after waiting over 12 months[4] per cent
Specialty			
Cardio-thoracic surgery	1.1	0	0
Ear nose and throat surgery	3.6	11	4
General surgery	1.7	7	1
Gynaecology	1.6	5	1
Neurosurgery	1.1	6	1
Opthalmology	3.2	6	1
Orthopaedic surgery	3.3	8	2
Plastic surgery	3.4	20	6
Urology	2.7	11	2
Vascular surgery	1.9	17	1
Other	1.0	2	0
All patients	2.3	9	2
Indicator procedure[5]			
Cataract extraction	4.0	6	2
Cholecystectomy	2.8	6	1
Coronary artery bypass graft	1.4	1	1
Cystoscopy	2.4	5	1
Haemorrhoidectomy	2.8	10	2
Hysterectomy	2.3	5	2
Inguinal herniorrhaphy	2.4	9	3
Myringoplasty	4.3	17	5
Myringotomy	2.3	4	0
Prostatectomy	4.1	14	4
Septoplasty	6.1	16	9
Tonsillectomy	4.5	10	6
Total hip replacement	3.9	8	6
Total knee replacement	4.7	8	4
Varicose veins stripping and ligation	5.7	18	5

1. The results are based on data from New South Wales, Victoria, Western Australia, South Australia, Tasmania, the Australian Capital Territory and the Northern Territory. Australian Capital Territory data were not available for the calculations in column 3. Victorian data were not used for the calculations in columns 2 and 3 as they are not comparable with data from other States and Territories.
2. Calculated as (patients on the waiting list at the census date)/[patients cleared (admitted or removed) during the survey period] for each specialty or procedure.
3. Calculated as (patients waiting >12 months at the census date)/(all patients on waiting lists at the census date) for each specialty or procedure.
4. Calculated as (patients admitted during survey period after waiting >12 months)/(all patients admitted during the survey period) for each specialty or procedure.
5. "Indicator procedures" comprise about one-third of the waiting list census and about one-quarter of elective surgery throughput. They comprise about one-third of patients waiting over 12 months at the census date and about one-third of patients admitted after waiting over 12 months.
Source: Australian Institute of Health and Welfare.

deliberate cost-shifting strategy as they may be an unavoidable consequence of the cap on public hospital budgets. The high levels of activity in private hospitals for procedures for which public waiting lists are long suggests that this factor has been persuasive for many patients.[108] Access to treatment for such procedures is clearly not being based on clinical need, but rather on ability to pay. This violates one of the foundation principles of Medicare and undermines the equity of the health system.

This issue highlights the ambiguous role of private insurance in the Australian health-care system. Such insurance is supposed to be an optional add-on to the universal Medicare scheme, paying for choice of surgeon and better quality hospital accommodation. But if this were really the case, private inpatients would pay only the extra costs of more comfortable accommodation and choice of surgeon. Instead, they pay for total accommodation costs[109] plus all other costs apart from the Medicare benefit (75 per cent of the MBS) for medical services. These contributions are estimated to save Medicare some A$ 2 billion per year. They are thus an important source of revenue for financing Medicare's commitments. People with private insurance know that they are paying much more than the costs of these optional add-ons. And they are prepared to do so mainly because it buys preferred access for elective surgery.[110] But this turns private insurance into a partial substitute for Medicare, buying access to elective surgery without the risk of having to wait longer than is clinically appropriate. One approach to finance health care, rather than selling preferred access to elective surgery could be to increase budgets for public hospitals to finance the expansion in treatment for public patients required to ensure that access is indeed on the basis of clinical need. However, such an approach has obvious implications in an environment of government expenditure restraint. Alternatively, further effort could be made to achieve greater efficiencies in the public hospital system to reduce inappropriate waiting times for elective surgery. For example, the recent introduction of casemix funding in Victoria has yielded considerable productivity increases; and there appears to be scope for gains from workforce reform. There is also scope for improved management of hospital waiting lists.

Workforce developments have also posed difficulties for expenditure restraint. The growing number of GPs (see Table 26) has increased service volumes correspondingly as the average number of services per full-time GP billing under the MBS has been stable; this number was 6 586 in FY 1984/85 and

6 588 FY 1992/93. And although there is no absolute way of assessing need, the Royal Australian College of General Practitioners estimates that there are now around 25 per cent more GPs than necessary. In the case of some medical specialities, the problem is undersupply, resulting in long waiting lists for public patients and high prices for private patients. A recent report (by Professor Baume) on factors affecting the quality and availability of surgical care in Australia concluded that there are not enough surgeons to meet reasonable standards of provision and that, given the training programmes of the Royal Australasian College of Surgeons (RACS), there will still be a shortage by the year 2001. Professor Baume concluded that the RACS exercised excessively tight control over the supply of trained surgeons.

The rising number of doctors also increased the number of prescriptions being written and hence, expenditure on pharmaceuticals. But the main factor pushing up expenditure on pharmaceuticals in recent years has been the shift to new higher priced drugs, especially for hypertension (ACE inhibitors), high cholesterol, ulcers and asthma, the areas in which the bulk of PBS expenditure occurs.[111] The impact of these increases has been more pronounced in Australia than in most other OECD countries because Australia has traditionally paid lower prices which resulted in a lower base for expenditure.

Another factor increasing expenditures on pharmaceuticals has been the increase in the proportion of the population eligible for concession cards. The number of people covered by concession cards increased from 3.884 million in June 1987 to 5.682 million in June 1992, an increase of 46 per cent. The reasons for this increase include population ageing, an increase in unemployment and government policy decisions. The major policy decision in this regard was to make the cards available to all aged pensioners, not just those with sufficiently limited means to be entitled to a full pension.

Directions for reform

The largely "top-down" approach to expenditure restraint so far adopted in Australia has been reasonably successful in containing health expenditures. Total health expenditures as a share of GDP have risen at only a slightly higher rate during the 1980s than the average for OECD countries and are currently only a little above the OECD average. But it seems unlikely that Australia will be able to continue to rely on this strategy in the long term. The most important element in the strategy has been the cap on funding for public hospitals, which has caused their share of total health expenditures to shrink markedly. But there are now signs in some States (especially the problems associated with queuing for elective surgery) that further budget cuts will seriously undermine their ability to honour the Medicare commitment to universal access to free, quality hospital care on the basis of clinical need, unless significant improvements in productivity can be achieved, as appears to be the case in Victoria recently. One of the other major planks in the "top-down" strategy, low pharmaceutical prices, also now seems to be under threat. Increasing use of new, high-priced drugs is driving up costs. And there is less scope to negotiate low pharmaceutical prices now that they are relatively low in Australia, at around 70 per cent of OECD average levels, and other countries more actively monitor the prices at which the drug companies are prepared to sell in Australia. Should Australia in future be unable to rely so heavily on these "top-down" ways of restraining the growth in health expenditures, it will have to find other approaches to restraining expenditure growth or face more rapid growth in health expenditures than most other OECD countries.

The driving force behind growth in health expenditures in Australia is volume growth in the fee-for-service sectors. Some microeconomic reforms have already been made to limit the scope of fee-for-service payment arrangements, but considerable scope remains to narrow the ambit of such payment arrangements. This section discusses some reforms which would further roll back fee-for-service payment systems as well as reduce the demarcations between funding for different forms of health care.

An extension of casemix funding to out-patient services[112]

Casemix funding involves payment for a treatment episode on the basis of average expected costs. If the treatment episode costs more than average, the service provider bears the cost while in the opposite case he keeps the savings. These payment arrangements remove the incentive that exists under fee-for-service to oversupply services to patients. As noted above, casemix payments have already replaced fee for service for obstetric services and multiple tests in pathology in order to reduce incentives for overservicing.

Duckett and Jackson (1993) propose extending casemix to the services provided by hospital out-patient departments.[113] The objective of this reform is to remove the incentive for public hospitals to shift costs to the MB scheme, the PB scheme and the private sector by closing, privatising or corporatising out-patient departments. This form of cost shifting has tended to undermine the quality of patient care and to increase the scope of the fee-for-service sector (and hence, overservicing of patients). It also undermines the effectiveness of the casemix funding reforms for public hospitals by providing them with a way to reduce costs at the expense of even higher costs elsewhere in the health sector.

The first and most straightforward episode type of care which Duckett and Jackson advocate being incorporated into DRG hospital funding is that surrounding admissions for elective surgery and childbirth. The hospital would be paid a set DRG-defined amount for all care provided during the periods directly before admission and after discharge. The more difficult episode type of care which they advocate being incorporated into hospital funding is that for patients with chronic illnesses across inpatient and out-patient settings. Hospital out-patient departments have developed many characteristics which are ideal for treating people with chronic conditions. Care in these departments is managed by a hospital medical specialist with access to other medical specialties, allied health professionals, medical records support, and specialised diagnostic and pharmacy services. And provided that the DRG payment covered all medical services during the episode of care, including those unrelated to the particular problem, cost shifting of difficult cases could be avoided.[114] The difficulty in so extending managed care, however, is that further research is required to establish appropriate payments for these bundles of care. Once the necessary information is available to make this extension, Duckett and Jackson advocate offering it as an option for patients: in exchange for (temporarily) foregoing their right to use the services of their choice of (fee-for-service) medical professional, patients would receive the advantages of the co-ordinated care of an out-patient department, including free access to allied health professionals and to pharmaceuticals.

Broad-banding health expenditure and purchaser-provider split

One option to address inefficiencies flowing from the split of functional responsibility is broad-banding of health expenditure. This would combine all public health funding in a single budget either at the Commonwealth or State level. For example, under broad-banding the Commonwealth government could set broad health policy objectives and allocate funds to States on a risk-weighted population basis. The States would be responsible for the public purchase of health-care services and would be accountable to the Commonwealth government. As the grants from the Commonwealth would be capped and States have limited own revenue sources, it would be necessary to cap the open-ended Medicare budgets for medical services and pharmaceuticals. Alternatively, a single budget for health care could be operated at the Commonwealth level.

In its simplest form, broad-banding would increase efficiency in the health sector by terminating the passive allocation of (supplier-induced) increasing amounts of resources to the fee-for-service sectors and by ending incentives to shift costs onto the Commonwealth.[115] But broad-banding also offers the possibility of introducing a full purchaser-provider split in public health expenditures, as in the United Kingdom and New Zealand. Funds could be passed down to district health authorities, which would be responsible for public-sector purchases of health care on behalf of their population. These purchasers would then be able to buy the combination of health care which they considered to offer the best value for their population and to use whatever form of contracting with providers proved to be most efficient. Purchasers would be accountable for their performance to either the States or the Commonwealth, depending on whether or not the States remained engaged in the financing of health-care expenditure. Although it is too early to draw definitive conclusions about such health-care reforms in other countries, there are already signs that UK hospitals are becoming more responsive to patients' needs and more efficient; that also seems to be the case in the State of Victoria.

GP payment arrangements

Irrespective of progress on the above reforms, the possibility of introducing blended payments for GPs, as in some other countries, could be considered. Under such arrangements, GPs would receive part of their incomes as capitation payments for specified outcomes. This would aim to reduce the importance of fee for service in GP incomes and hence the incentive to oversupply medical services. GP geographical registration would also be worth considering to overcome the shortages in rural areas and reduce the oversupply in urban areas.

V. Conclusions

The current economic upswing, unusually weak during its first two years, gathered considerable strength in the course of 1994. With plant and equipment investment finally taking off, dwelling investment remaining strong and private consumption and public investment accelerating, real GDP is likely to have risen by over 5 per cent in 1994, among the fastest growth rates in the OECD region. From the December quarter 1993 onwards, employment began to respond vigorously to the strengthening of output growth, with some 265 000 new jobs being created during 1994 alone, allaying the fears of "jobless growth" that were widespread in the earlier phase of the recovery. The unemployment rate declined rapidly, from a rate of around 11 per cent – which persisted over nearly 1½ years until November 1993 – to just under 9 per cent at the end of 1994. And long-term unemployment even fell somewhat faster than overall unemployment. But with continuing labour market slack, wage inflation has continued to be subdued. This, together with robust labour productivity growth, underpinned low inflation. Both "headline" inflation and measures of underlying inflation remained at 2 per cent or less in 1994, for the third consecutive year. Despite strong export growth, a surge in imports raised the current account deficit to around 5 per cent of GDP in late 1994.

High output growth during the second half of 1994 is likely to have continued into 1995. But fiscal consolidation and measures of monetary restriction in 1994 and assumed further interest rate increases should slow the growth of GDP closer to that of potential output which is accelerating owing to strong growth in business investment. With total employment projected to grow by about 3 per cent in 1995 and 1996, the unemployment rate may fall below 8 per cent in 1996. The external sector is projected again to make a negative contribution to growth in 1995 but, with the breaking of the drought in the Eastern States and slowing growth in imports, to make a positive contribution in the following year. On OECD projections, the current account deficit may, therefore, rise to almost 6 per cent of GDP in 1995 but ease to 5¼ per cent of GDP in 1996. With projected output growth above its potential, there is a risk of increasing inflationary pressures as the economy's capacity limits are reached.

The Reserve Bank of Australia (RBA) changed the course of monetary policy towards restriction in mid-1994 in order to forestall risks of overheating. The official cash rate was raised in three pre-emptive moves by a cumulative 275 basis points between August and December 1994, with the two most recent moves being both earlier and bigger than markets had anticipated. It is, however, difficult to judge whether these moves were sufficiently early or large to secure the authorities' objective of keeping the average rate of *underlying* inflation at around 2 to 3 per cent over the cycle. The rise in inflation expectations during the past year – especially as indicated by the gap between index-linked and nominal government bond yields – suggests that the private sector remains to be convinced about the authorities' capacity to meet their medium-term inflation objective.

Experience in other countries shows that the credibility of monetary policy can be gained ultimately by achieving a good inflation record, which takes considerable time. The progress to date in building monetary policy credibility could be eroded if underlying inflation were to exceed the authorities' objective for more than a brief period. And it is in periods of buoyant economic activity that the authorities' commitment to low inflation is really tested. The strong output growth of recent months, the associated rapidly declining slack in the economy, and the long and uncertain lags between changes in monetary policy settings and their impact on output and inflation suggest that the authorities will need to remain vigilant regarding the risks to the inflation outlook. The interest rate rises so far have been designed to minimise these risks. But the authorities' investment to date in building policy credibility, and the scope for it to be undermined quickly, should be borne in mind when considering monetary policy settings in coming months. Maintaining low inflation will also be made easier if the parties to wage and salary negotiations adopt a responsible attitude.

Fiscal policy should make a greater contribution to slowing growth in aggregate demand to more sustainable levels. The Commonwealth Government has acknowledged this in announcing its intention to effect a structural tightening of policy in the 1995 Budget, so as to bring the budget into surplus by

FY 1996/97. In taking such action, temporary measures, such as a tax surcharge, should be avoided as they do not reduce the structural deficit and risk having little effect on aggregate demand because they might well be largely offset by lower private savings. Such measures also reduce economic efficiency by creating uncertainty about government policies. Instead, structural deficit reductions should be sought through further spending restraint, especially if associated with improved efficiency and, if necessary, revenue increases, preferably as a result of base broadening.

The Commonwealth Government is now in the second year of the four-year budget consolidation programme it announced in the 1993 Budget. On current projections this programme, whose degree of adjustment compares favourably with those of most other OECD countries, will reduce the budget deficit from 3.7 per cent of GDP in FY 1993/94 to an estimated 2.6 per cent in FY 1994/95. The faster than anticipated revenue growth in FY 1994/95 will flow through into faster deficit reduction in later years, meaning that the previously projected deficit target of just under 1 per cent of GDP in FY 1996/97 should be significantly improved upon. In the OECD's view, the major risk to this outlook is that the growth rates underlying the projections – averaging 4 to $4^{1}/_{2}$ per cent a year – may not be sustainable given the closing of the output gap. However, this risk should be viewed in the context of the Government's commitment to take the measures needed to achieve a Commonwealth budget surplus in FY 1996/97.

While net government debt remains lower in Australia than in most other OECD countries, the debt-to-GDP ratio is projected to increase to a peak of 27 per cent in 1996 before declining again. The recently foreshadowed fiscal package can be expected to improve this outlook but nonetheless recent developments underline the importance of maintaining medium-term fiscal policy objectives. This involves taking a view on the desired evolution of public debt over coming decades. Although the Australian Government undoubtedly has the scope to go on increasing its indebtedness over successive business cycles, this would undermine the objective of maintaining and lifting national saving. Such an approach would be likely to result in high structural current account deficits and rising external liabilities. This could affect credit ratings and investor sentiment and expose the economy to greater risks of instability. For an economy subject to large swings in its terms of trade, a low public debt policy would appear to be prudent. And in view of the future public expenditure commitments associated with an ageing population structure, vigorous action to increase public saving over the next two decades will probably be required if high levels of public debt are subsequently to be avoided.

Over the longer run, faster non-inflationary growth can be achieved only through fostering the economy's productive potential. To this end, important structural policy reforms have been implemented over recent years, which have been discussed in previous OECD *Economic Surveys of Australia.* Further steps undertaken during the past twelve months focused primarily on industrial relations, the functioning of labour markets and on enhancing domestic competition through the implementation of the "Hilmer Committee" proposals.

Reform of the industrial relations system in Australia continues to be a high priority of the Government. The thrust of reforms is to continue the shift from the previous system of a more centralised determination of wages and work conditions to enterprise bargaining. This shift will provide employees and employers flexibility to negotiate mutually advantageous terms and conditions of employment. With this flexibility, it is expected that changes in working arrangements can be made which will increase productivity and thereby provide a basis for higher real wages. The latest development in this domain is the Industrial Relations Reform Act 1993 (in force since 30 March 1994), which has introduced significant changes to promote enterprise bargaining. In particular, so called "enterprise flexibility agreements" have increased the scope for non-unionised workplaces to formalise enterprise agreements in the federal system. The Act also reinforced the award safety net by stressing the Industrial Relations Commission's obligation to ensure that employees are protected by awards which set fair and enforceable minimum wages and conditions of employment which are maintained at a relevant level. The Act also established an award review process which is intended to help ensure that awards are adaptable to the needs of both employers and employees. Critics have argued that the co-existence of awards and bargaining is an impediment to enterprise agreements being reached. Moreover, they argue that the new legislation remains very complex and overly prescriptive. The Government, on the other hand, considers that the safety net, together with the "no disadvantage test", provides an environment conducive to the shift to enterprise bargaining, maintaining social consensus, and ensuring that the focus of bargaining is on achieving sustainable productivity improvements. In any case, there is no question that the labour market needs to be capable of adapting to the challenges of a changing world and stronger international competition in the 1990s. This requires that the impetus behind the shift to enterprise bargaining must be maintained and strengthened.

The labour market programmes and related reforms announced in the *Working Nation* White Paper are in line with recommendations made by the OECD *Jobs Study*. This Study stresses the role active labour-market policies can play in assisting re-employment if the measures are well-designed and targeted on specific client groups, such as the long-term unemployed. The largest element of the package, the *Job Compact,* is focused on persons on unemployment allowance for more than 18 months on the grounds that prolonged joblessness is demoralising for those affected and leads to loss of skills and of competitiveness in the labour market. Complementing the employment measures are some significant education and training measures, including a substantial expansion in the number of entry-level training places available and the introduction of the training wage. These measures, in combination with others outside the *Working Nation* package, are intended to improve Australia's skill base and hence growth potential. The extent to which these measures contribute to the ultimate goal of reducing the unemployment rate to 5 per cent by the end of the decade is an empirical question. Specifically, the net impact on employment will depend in part on how much the improved employability of the long-term unemployed results in enhanced labour market efficiency, leading to reduced wage pressures and a higher level of employment than would otherwise be the case.

Another pillar of the *Working Nation* package is changes in income support arrangements, effective as from 1 July 1995. The changes aim at minimising the adverse effect of the so-called "poverty trap" (or "dependency trap") on labour supply. Such a "trap" arises at low income levels when the interaction of taxation and the withdrawal of social benefits results in no or very little additional disposable income from extra work. Even with this reform, low-income earners will continue to face quite high effective marginal tax rates. But the changed system will ease the financial penalties associated hitherto with the taking of part-time or temporary jobs and is therefore to be welcomed.

The centre-piece of planned microeconomic reform is the Hilmer Committee proposals to enhance competition. The Commonwealth has to date adopted a co-operative approach with the States and Territories concerning the implementation of these reforms but has signalled that it is prepared to implement them unilaterally if the States do not agree to co-operate at the April 1995 Council of Australian Government's (COAG) meeting. A study assessing the benefits of the reforms is currently underway and the results will be available for consideration at that meeting.

Some of the Federal government's recent decisions on microeconomic reform unfortunately may not be seen as sitting easily with its support of competition policy reform and with the substantial progress that has been made on the reform task more generally. One example is the continued exemption of liner shipping conferences from certain provisions of the Trade Practices Act. Another is that part of the *Working Nation* programme assigns greater weight to industry development in procurement guidelines. In practice, however, Commonwealth purchasing decisions will continue to be made primarily on a price performance basis in an open and transparent tendering process.

One area where microeconomic reform promises large returns is the health-care system, the subject of this *Survey*'s special chapter. Australia has been able to contain health-care spending as a share of national income to roughly the OECD average, while at the same time the health status of the population has improved significantly over recent decades. Its health-care system – which combines both public and private arrangements and guarantees every citizen access to comprehensive care – has contributed to this improvement, and the public has been generally satisfied with the service provided. Growth in health-care expenditure has been restrained mainly through a cap on budgets for public sector hospitals. Although the government's use of its monopsony power to keep medical-specific inflation low has also contributed, this was more than offset by high growth in medical-service volumes in the ambulatory sector, which are mainly supplied on a fee-for-service basis, and in quantities of drugs prescribed.

This approach to expenditure restraint has undermined efficiency in the health-care sector. Expenditure restraint has been focused where the use of capped budgets made it possible, not necessarily where resources were being used least efficiently. Efficiency has been further jeopardised by the strategies adopted by hospitals in the face of capped budgets to shift costs onto the ambulatory, private hospital and out-of-hospital pharmaceuticals sectors, where the Commonwealth government provides subsidies on a fee-for-service basis. These strategies, which involve reducing the amount of medical care offered in public hospitals that can be offered elsewhere as much as possible, and thereby forcing patients to seek substitute care as private patients, have lowered the quality of patient care and the efficiency of service delivery. Waiting times for non-urgent surgery for public hospital patients have also encouraged them to seek private care. This has resulted in access to some forms of treatment being available more on the basis of ability to pay than of clinical need, contrary to one of the founding principles of Medicare, the universal public health-care scheme. Queues for elective surgery are the main source of public dissatisfaction with Medicare.

While the cap on public hospital budgets has undoubtedly made an important contribution to restraining the growth in health expenditures, the cap cannot be maintained indefinitely unless significant ongoing improvements in productivity can be achieved. Indeed, there are already signs in some States that service will be adversely affected if current arrangements remain unchanged. New ways of restraining expenditure growth need to be found. To be effective, these will have to focus on the root cause of expenditure pressures – fee-for-service payment arrangements for medical services and capped hospital budgets without incentives to improve the efficiency of service delivery.

Fee-for-service payments for doctors encourage them to oversupply services in an environment in which patients – and even doctors themselves, albeit to a lesser extent – are uncertain about the precise clinical benefits of a given procedure and at the same time are faced with virtually zero marginal costs at the point of delivery of services. This has been recognised in recent Australian reforms which have sought to limit the oversupply of medical services under fee-for-service arrangements. These reforms include moving to payments for an episode of care – otherwise known as casemix funding – in areas where there has been unusually high growth in service volumes, and establishing a peer review mechanism to monitor overservicing by individual doctors. Private insurance funds are being given the capacity to counter over-servicing by progressively introducing casemix funding. However, there remains considerable scope for further reform of the fee-for-service sectors. A useful extension of casemix funding would be to the services provided by the hospital out-patient departments. This would close the main conduit for cost shifting and would help to limit the extent of fee-for-service arrangements. It would also reinforce the effectiveness of the casemix funding reforms for public hospitals – which were pioneered by the State of

Victoria and are being followed by other States – by preventing them from cutting their costs through cost shifting.

A more fundamental reform worth considering would be to combine public health budgets into a consolidated budget in the hands of a single agent or series of agents – and to strengthen the purchasing role of these agents. The agents might be the Commonwealth, State or area levels of administration. This would greatly reduce cost shifting pressures and would permit public health-care expenditures to be allocated more efficiently. The casemix-based method of funding public hospitals can be seen as a first significant move in enhancing the purchasing function.

Rising cost pressures and a trend decline in the number of subscribers have the potential to eroded the profitability of private health insurance funds (although the funds have in fact increased their reserves in recent years). Insurance reforms before the Parliament in early 1995 sought to allow funds to offer cheaper insurance cover by permitting them to enter into purchaser-provider agreements (contracts) with a restricted range of hospitals. Funds will also be permitted to offer products which cover the full cost of medical services as long as these are based on purchaser-provider agreements with doctors. These reforms are welcome as they would expand the range of insurance products available to consumers. In considering future reforms, however, it would be useful to have regard to whether the intended role of private insurance is as a substitute for, or a top-up to, public arrangements.

In conclusion, Australia is now at the point in the economic cycle where the authorities' resolve to achieve sustainable growth and to lock in low inflation will be tested. Economic growth appears to be slowing from the very rapid rate experienced in 1994, but is likely to need to slow further if a build-up of inflationary pressures is to be avoided. The anticipatory tightening of monetary policy since mid-1994 is a welcome sign of the authorities' determination to keep inflation low. Fiscal policy settings will also contribute to a slowing in aggregate demand growth as the deficit reductions already programmed unfold. The need to slow aggregate demand growth to more sustainable rates provides the authorities with an ideal opportunity, as intended, to reinforce the current fiscal consolidation programme. An adequate response would facilitate the task of monetary policy and would contribute to a lasting reduction in Australia's current account deficit. The rewards from containing inflationary pressures over the next two to three years would be substantial. The authorities' low inflation policies would gain credibility and the economic expansion should be prolonged. Together with the stepped-up effort in implementing structural reform, macroeconomic stability promises Australians a durable improvement in living standards.

Notes

1. If not indicated otherwise, all references to GDP are to GDP(A), which is the average of the expenditure, income and production measures of GDP.

2. Fiscal years start 1 July.

3. The Australian Bureau of Statistics (ABS) calculates trend estimates by smoothing the seasonally-adjusted series using a statistical procedure based on centred Henderson moving averages. The purpose of this practice is to extract the underlying behaviour of the series by purging irregular components from the data which may have remained even after seasonal adjustment.

4. The drought may reduce overall economic growth in FY 1994/95 by $3/4$ percentage point.

5. See Reserve Bank of Australia (1994), *1994 Report and Financial Statements,* Sydney, p. 8.

6. However, upward revisions to private business investment since the March quarter National Accounts indicate that business investment has been making a contribution to economic activity since mid-1992. In the June quarter 1994 National Accounts, private business investment data were revised upwards following the incorporation of the FY 1991/92 taxation statistics and other benchmark data in the National Accounts. The September quarter 1994 National Accounts saw a further upward revision of A\$ 2.3 billion to total private business investment in FY 1993/94, following the incorporation of data on the growth in new businesses in FY 1993/94. Of this increase, around A\$ 2.2 billion was attributed to upward revisions to plan and equipment investment.

7. See Mills, Morling and Tease (1994).

8. Potential output and the output gap are notional concepts that do not take account of the adjustments that occur in the economy as output moves towards its potential and which can themselves increase the economy's potential output. To derive estimates of the output gap, it is necessary to make explicit or implicit assumptions about the use of capital and labour as output in the economy expands. Usually these assumptions are based on historical relationships, which are unable to reflect the wide range of dynamic influences in the economy; such as, the effect of changing product and factor prices on employment and investment decisions. The choice of assumptions has a marked effect on the final estimates of the output gap. Thus, by using past growth in capital stock, the OECD's estimates are significantly affected by the decline in business investment in the early 1990s. The estimates do not, for example, take account of anecdotal evidence which suggests that capital productivity is increasing owing to workplace change. If this is the case, capacity might be higher than a

literal reading of the capital stock data suggests, which would increase estimates of potential output and the output gap.

9. See Wooden, Fan and Sloan (1994).

10. This Beveridge curve differs from earlier work in that the vacancy data have been adjusted for a break in the series in 1983. Vacancies have also been lagged by two quarters to remove some of the cyclical dynamics from the curve caused by the fact that vacancies rise before unemployment falls.

11. See Chapter III below.

12. The Australian Industrial Relations Commission's September 1994 Safety Net Adjustments and Review decision made available two further increases – A$ 8 per week not before September 1994 at the enterprise level and not before March 1995 at the award level. Another A$ 8 per week is available not before September 1995 at the enterprise level and at the award level, no earlier than March 1996, for those groups unable to reach enterprise agreements.

13. Downward pressures on import prices are expected to remain as tariff barriers continue to fall (especially in the textiles, clothing and footwear industries).

14. The Treasury underlying inflation series excludes from the CPI mortgage and consumer debt charges as well as volatile items including fresh fruits and vegetables, meat and seafoods, tobacco and alcohol, petrol, items with a marked seasonal pattern, such as holiday travel and accommodation and clothing, and goods and services mostly provided by the public sector. The Treasury measure thus only retains about 50 per cent of the CPI basket.

15. Of course, this measure is not ideal, since factors other than inflation expectations may explain part of the difference between the return on non-indexed and index-linked bonds. One factor which may distort the comparison of yields is the relative illiquidity of the Australian market for indexed bonds, its volume being less than one-tenth of that for non-indexed bonds. Moreover, the differential between yields of similar maturity may reflect not only mean inflation expectations but also a premium for uncertainty about the level of future inflation, and this premium may rise when market volatility increases. Also, maturities of indexed and non-indexed bonds often do not match exactly. Moreover, inflation expectations of those who make savings and investment decisions may differ from expectations of financial markets. But even with these caveats, the non-indexed/indexed bond yield differential contains useful information about expected inflation.

16. The decline in volumes will be partially offset by improvements in prices, which will limit the actual impact on the current account deficit.

17. *Cf.* Governor B.W. Fraser (1994).

18. However, once the disequilibrating effects from the recent wave of financial innovation have petered out, the classical money-price relationship as long-run anchor to monetary policy might re-establish itself. See Orden and Fisher (1993).

19. Here defined as ten-year Treasury bonds.

20. Simulations with the OECD INTERLINK model of Australia suggest relatively long lags between changes in the monetary policy setting and the full response of output and inflation, even with a floating exchange rate. For example, a change in the Australian three-month

interest rates by one percentage point has only a minor impact on output and inflation after one year. The model shows only about one-third of the total inflation effect three years after the change in policy.

21. Since January 1990, the RBA has announced every change in the cash rate and comments upon it in order to make monetary policy more transparent and to avoid the potential for confusion of the earlier practice.

22. The RBA affects short-term interest rates indirectly through open-market operations of (mainly) government paper. It sells them to or purchases them from those recognised dealers in the money market who have access to the lender-of-last-resort facility and who form the market for official overnight funds. The so-determined official overnight fund rate then spreads to the cash rate in the – much larger – unofficial money market. A stable relationship between official and unofficial cash rates – cf. Elliot and Bewley (1994) – implies that the RBA can control the market-determined unofficial overnight funds interest rate with high precision.

23. Simulations with the OECD INTERLINK model suggest that – everything else unchanged – the cumulative increase in the cash rate by 275 basis points would bring the private consumption deflator nearly ½ percentage point below its baseline value after two years and a little more than 1 percentage point after three years.

24. The analysis of published credit series is complicated by the fact that they contain numerous statistical breaks due to the reclassification of bank loans.

25. Everything else unchanged, in particular unchanged terms of trade.

26. Broad money equals M3 plus borrowings from the private sector by non-bank financial institutions less the latter's holdings of currency and bank deposits. In general, broad money follows movements of M3.

27. The comparison of Australian ex ante real interest rates with US ex post real rates can be justified by the fact that the United States' authorities have a much longer record in keeping inflation relatively low. Hence, for the United States the ex post real bond rate is likely to be a more sensible proxy for ex ante real long-term interest rates than for Australia.

28. To reduce the impact of outliers in the data, the median of survey-based consumer inflation expectations data has been used here instead of the mean. The latter is often employed by analysts and shows a more pronounced rise in expected inflation during 1994 (by 1¼ percentage point from end-1993 to end-1994) than the median. However, it seems that 1 to 3 per cent of the population expect the price level to increase by 21 to 100 per cent over the next twelve months, which may weaken the mean's meaningfulness.

29. For many countries neither surveys of price expectations nor indexed bonds exist. Therefore nominal interest rates have been deflated by trend inflation expectations, which have been approximated by the low frequency component of the GDP deflator using a Hodrick-Prescott filter.

30. In the framework of an error-correction model a long-run trend relationship has been specified between real long-term interest rates and key long-run determinants together with short-term deviations in actual real rates from their trend levels. A multi-country approach has been adopted which restricts the parameters of the long-run trend relationship to be equal for all countries. This has the implication that in the case that domestic economic

fundamentals were equal in all countries, then all countries' real rates would converge to a common level. However, no restrictions have been placed on the short-term dynamics. It is intended to present the results in a forthcoming OECD Economics Department Working Paper.

31. Proxied by a variable which aims at capturing domestic financial market volatility as a measure of undiversifiable risk.

32. This variable equals the difference of a ten-year moving average of inflation and the Hodrick-Prescott trend inflation. In Australia, the former is still higher than the latter, putting a positive risk premium on top of the (unobserved) risk-free real return on capital.

33. Two other variables also turned out to be statistically significant in explaining real bond rates over the sample period. These variables are the change in the domestic real short-term interest rate (as a proxy for monetary tightening) and the change in inflation (as a proxy for expected future tightening); both have important positive short-term effects on long-term real interest rates in general. However, they contribute less to the explanation of developments in real rates, in particular in the first half of 1994 when both short-term interest rates and inflation remained steady. Exchange rate variations were also identified as significant, but the appreciation of the Australian dollar in 1994 rather tended to slow the increase in real interest rates in the logic of the model. Finally, government deficits as an indicator of fiscal sustainability could not be found statistically significant for the explanation of real long-term interest rates.

34. This section draws heavily on the National Fiscal Outlook 1995. As in that publication, budget balances are adjusted unless otherwise indicated, to remove privatisation proceeds and the effects of Commonwealth borrowing on behalf of, and lending to, the States and Territories.

35. Including privatisation proceeds, the general government budget balance deteriorated from a surplus of 1.6 per cent of GDP in FY 1988/89 to a peak deficit of 5.0 per cent of GDP in FY 1992/93. Privatisation proceeds by level of government have been the following as a per cent of GDP:

	87/88	88/89	89/90	90/91	91/92	92/93	93/94
Commonwealth	0.4	0.2	0.3	0.0	0.1	0.2	0.6
States	0.0	0.0	0.0	0.2	0.0	0.3	0.2

There were no privatisation before FY 1987/88.

36. The previous cyclical high as a per cent of GDP for the Commonwealth budget deficit were 3.6 per cent in FY 1983/84 and 2.8 per cent in FY 1975/76.

37. References to "States" include States and Territories.

38. Social security outlays rose from 5.5 per cent of GDP in FY 1988/89 to 7.5 per cent in FY 1992/93, with unemployment payments rising from 0.9 per cent of GDP to 1.8 per cent over the same period.

39. The strong lift in State own revenue in FY 1993/94 was mainly due to higher stamp duty collections resulting from increased property and share-market transactions.

40. Fiscal data in this sub-section are unadjusted. They are on a budget basis and refer only to the Commonwealth Government. Privatisation proceeds are, therefore, included in the data, unless otherwise indicated.

41. These were forecast to cost A$ 1.7 billion in FY 1993/94.

42. These projections are derived from the National Fiscal Outlook (NFO) 1995. They are based on assumed growth rates which lie midway between those presented in the NFO 1995. The assumed growth rates are (percentage changes):

	1994/95	1995/96	1996/97	1997/98
Real GDP	5½	4¼	4	3¾

43. This compares with a State budget surplus in FY 1993/94 of 0.2 per cent of GDP. This surplus mainly reflected one-off factors, including a A$ 1.2 to 2 billion payment to the State of Victoria's budget from the Transport Accident Commission and the Australian Bureau of Statistics' decision to treat the FY 1993/94 payment of A$ 1.3 billion of deferred superannuation liabilities in Victoria on an accrual accounting basis. This involved the allocation of the A$ 1.3 billion payment to recorded outlays across the previous 15 years (*i.e.* the years in which the liabilities were actually deferred), rather than treating the item as a financing transaction in FY 1993/94.

44. For both the Commonwealth and the States, net debt as a percentage of GDP is now also higher than it was in the early 1980s.

45. Growth in the OECD projections is similar to the low growth scenario (3.75 per cent in FY 1995/96) in the NFO 1995.

46. Fitzgerald (1993), p. 11.

47. Examples are the Treasury Macroeconomic model (TRYM) and the Murphy model [*cf.* Murphy (1988)]. Estimates of the OECD Secretariat, which are markedly higher, are presented in Table 3 above.

48. This refers to working conditions in the broadest sense and not just to the issue of flexible wages. Indeed, a study by Coelli, Fahrer and Lindsay (1994) suggests that Australian wage flexibility in the 1980s – as measured by wage dispersion across ten sectors – has been rather high by international standards, in spite of the centralised wage setting system. Actually, Australian wage dispersion was found to be on the scale of that in the United States, a country which is widely considered to have a flexible labour market. Moreover, the study did not find a strong relationship between the degree of centralisation of wage setting institutions and wage dispersion across countries. An increase in the dispersion of earnings in Australia from 1978 onwards has also been reported in OECD (1993), *Employment Outlook,* Chapter 5. Moreover, the OECD (1994) *Jobs Study, Evidence and Explanations,* Part II: "The adjustment potential of the labour market", Chapter 6, Section III, found Australian employment protection to be low (and freedom to dismiss high) relative to European OECD countries and Japan.

49. Australia's system of wage awards – organised by craft and occupation and based on compulsory arbitration and conciliation – specifies *minimum* wages and conditions of work for most categories of labour. It is thus illegal to employ a worker at a wage or on other

terms which are less favourable than the relevant award, irrespective of whether a worker is union member or not. Awards based on compulsory arbitration are made by the Australian Industrial Relations Commission and by industrial relations tribunals in five of the six States. In the other State, Victoria, the Employee Relations Commission has the power to make awards with the consent of all parties.

50.   Further background on the Prices and Incomes Accord and the shift towards a more decentralised industrial relations system is included in OECD, *Economic Survey of Australia 1993/94,* Chapter IV.

51.   See OECD, *Economic Survey of Australia 1993/94,* Chapter IV.

52.   In mid-1990, some 31 per cent of wage and salary earners were covered by federal awards. Since then, there have been significant changes that have had an effect on award coverage, including the abolition of State awards in Victoria, and substantial movement of wage and salary earners in Victoria to the federal award system. However, no reliable measures of current award coverage are available.

53.   Agreed reductions are also allowed if these are judged not to be against the public interest, for example, as part of a strategy for dealing with a short term business crisis and revival. However, Sloan (1994) expresses the view that downward flexibility of pay, for example when an enterprise suffers a slump in the demand for its products, is only a theoretical possibility with little chances of ever being implemented in practice.

54.   For example, in Victoria, where the reforms have been most radical, no data are collected. A current estimate is that State awards presently cover about 50 per cent of Australian wage and salary earners.

55.   Stewart (1994), p. 140.

56.   ''Many parts of the Act have now become all but unintelligible to any but those with substantial experience with complex legal documents'' [Stewart (1994), p. 159].

57.   In a widely publicised case, a metal-workers trade union sought orders from the Commission directing a company to negotiate with it for an enterprise agreement. The orders were granted, despite the fact that the employees of the company were not trade union members and did not want the union to negotiate on their behalf. An appeal, supported by the Commonwealth Government, against the decision to grant the orders was upheld.

58.   Awards cover a variety of groups consistent with the definition of ''industry'' in the Act; including industries, sections of industries, occupations and unions. There are relatively few ''craft'' awards. Most importantly, there are many single-employer awards. There are about 1 400 active multi-employer wages and conditions awards and about 1 400 single-employer awards in the federal system.

59.   The Accord VII agreement (reached in February 1993 and reaffirmed on 1 June 1994) between the Federal Government and the Australian Council of Trade Unions (ACTU) included provision for three A$ 8 per week safety net wage increases for employees genuinely unable to achieve a wage increase through workplace bargaining. In its October 1993 Review of Wage Fixing Principles decision, the AIRC awarded an A$ 8 per week increase in supplementary payments prescribed in minimum rates awards, to be absorbed against overaward payments or increases through enterprise bargaining. Subsequently, the AIRC's September 1994 Safety Net Adjustments and Review decision widened

access to the October 1993 increase and made available two further A$ 8 increases over two years, initially at enterprise level and subsequently at award level, in line with the approach agreed between the Government and the ACTU in Accord VII. The modest size of the increases (each equivalent to around 1.3 per cent of average weekly ordinary time earnings for a full-time adult) and their phased implementation will ensure that they are consistent with the Accord commitment to maintain Australia's inflation at a rate comparable with the rates of its major trading partners.

60. See, for example, Committee on Employment Opportunities (1993*a*), p. 6.

61. *Cf.* Committee on Employment Opportunities (1993*b*), p. 24.

62. OECD (1993), *Employment Outlook,* Chapter 3, Section B.4, presents evidence for the relatively low educational attainment of long-term unemployed in a number of countries, including Australia.

63. *Ibid.,* p. 108.

64. The Government's programme is laid out in *Working Nation, The White Paper on Employment and Growth,* Canberra, May 1994, which is the first White Paper on employment since 1945. Details on the rationale behind the programme and on its various initiatives are given in the companion volume *Working Nation, Policies and Programs,* Canberra, May 1994.

65. Empirical analysis puts Australia into the group of countries where the effect of active labour market programmes on wage moderation appears positive and statistically significant. However, these results are not very robust. See OECD (1993), *Employment Outlook,* Chapter 2, Tables 2.3 and 2.4.

66. *Cf.* OECD (1994), *The OECD Jobs Study, Facts-Analysis-Strategies,* Part III.7 and OECD (1993), *Employment Outlook,* Chapter 2.

67. Under the *JOBSTART* programme employers can receive wage subsidies of between A$ 910 and A$ 9 470 (including bonus) for employing eligible job seekers. Over 227 000 long-term unemployed are reported to have been hired by employers with JOBSTART subsidies in the three years FY 1991/92, FY 1992/93 and FY 1993/94. Of these, over one-half have obtained lasting employment.

68. The Training Guarantee, which was introduced in 1990 and required all but small firms to spend a minimum of 1.5 per cent of their payroll on training, has been suspended in recognition of the improved awareness of and commitment to training by Australian firms, and the expected increase in training places arising from the National Training Wage and the expansion of entry-level training.

69. Under the present system there are huge disincentives for the unemployed to accept part-time or temporary jobs. Single persons with maximum rent assistance gain nothing if their part-time earnings rise from A$ 85 per week to A$ 212 per week. A married couple with one spouse in part-time employment would receive the same disposable income from earnings of A$ 338 per week as they would from earnings of A$ 95 per week of income [*cf.* Committee on Employment Opportunities (1993*b*), p. 24]. Hence, income in these respective ranges are effectively taxed at 100 per cent. The reason why effective marginal tax rates are so high for people earning private income and receiving unemployment

133

payments is that Australia has a targeted welfare system: as private income rises, welfare payments fall.

70. See also OECD (1994), *Economic Survey of Australia 1993/94,* Parts III and IV, and *Assessing Structural Reform: Lessons for the Future,* Part II, Paris.

71. However, the *Open-Skies Agreement* with New Zealand of 1992, which envisaged enhanced competition in domestic aviation through the staged establishment of a single trans-Tasman aviation market, suffered a major setback in October 1994, when the Federal Government announced its decision not to proceed with certain elements of its memorandum of under-standing with the New Zealand Government on the development of a unified domestic aviation market. The practical effect was to prevent Air New Zealand from entering the domestic aviation market. The open skies arrangements for trans-Tasman operations was not affected by the Federal Government's decision, and the beyond rights contained in the memorandum of understanding remain in place.

72. *Cf.* Hilmer, F.G., M. Rayner and G. Taperell (The Independent Committee of Inquiry) (1993), *National Competition Policy,* AGPS, Canberra. A brief overview of the recommen-dations can be found in OECD, *Economic Survey of Australia 1993/94,* Part III, Paris, 1994.

73. However, in October 1994, the Federal Government decided that members of international liner shipping conferences operating in Australia's liner trades would continue to be granted limited exemption from the competition provisions of the Trade Practices Act.

74. These are general-purpose, as opposed to tied, grants. It is estimated that States spend up to 30 per cent of their Financial Assistance Grants on health care.

75. "Public" hospitals refer to "Medicare-designated" hospitals in this *Survey.* Hospitals owned by the public sector are referred to as "publicly-owned" hospitals.

76. No single out-of-pocket expense from the difference between the Medicare rebate and the Schedule fee should exceed A$ 28.10 and, in aggregate, these out-of-pocket expenses should not exceed A$ 258.10 in a year. These limits are indexed annually.

77. Although this is not so for some specialists – see below.

78. This is calculated as the product of the average cost sharing and coverage ratios.

79. AIHW (1994), pp. 8-9. OECD data for life expectancy at age 60 are unavailable before 1960.

80. From all causes except external causes (which includes motor vehicle accidents) and suicides.

81. Perinatal mortality is defined as the sum of stillbirths and deaths within 28 days of birth, expressed as a percentage of all births.

82. Infant mortality is defined as deaths within the first year of life, expressed as a percentage of live births.

83. This discussion about Aboriginal health draws extensively from AIHW (1994), pp. 26-36.

84. Havard Caunter survey, which appeared in Blendon, R.J., *et al.* (1990), pp. 185-192. Caution is required in interpreting these single-observation results, despite the care taken by the Havard Caunter team to ensure that the responses were comparable.

85. The major source of dissatisfaction in the United States was with the coverage of health insurance while in Sweden, the main concern was with waiting lists and the impersonal way in which care was delivered. Since the Caunter survey, there has been a dramatic drop in waiting lists and improvement in service in Sweden.

86. TQA Research Pty Ltd. (1994).

87. Definitional differences, however, make international comparisons difficult.

88. The Japanese data are, however, distorted by the practice of medical practioners supplying pharmaceuticals directly.

89. *Ibid.*

90. Medical-specific inflation is the excess of medical price inflation over general inflation.

91. A purchaser-provider split refers to a situation in which publicly funded health services are purchased from competing suppliers instead of being funded directly, usually on the basis of historical allocations. In the Australian context, the purchaser-provider split is limited to the funding of public hospitals. Contracts between government purchasers and public hospitals use casemix, otherwise known as Diagnostic-Related Group (DRG) episodes of care, to measure output. Under this system, each treatment available in a public hospital is classified to a DRG on the basis of its average expected cost of treatment.

92. Expenditure on public hospitals is estimated by the Australian Institute of Health and Welfare (AIHW) from the records of expenditure of state, territory and Commonwealth health authorities. The medical fees paid by private patients to the treating doctor are not included in the cost of public hospitals.

93. Expenditure on private hospitals is estimated from the revenue received from patient accommodation, operating-theatre and other fees. The fees which private patients pay for the medical services of the treating doctor are not included; taking these fees into account, total spending on private hospitals probably increased even faster.

94. This programme, which also provides support services to younger disabled people who are not in residential care, aims to enhance opportunities for people to lead fulfilling lives and to avoid inappropriate admission to institutions.

95. Under direct (otherwise known as ''bulk'') billing (to Medicare), the doctor accepts the Medicare rebate (85 per cent of the MBS) as full payment for the service provided. As at December 1993, 67 per cent of doctors, most of whom were GPs, were direct billing.

96. Fees for individual tests were also cut.

97. Oxley *et al.,* 1995, p. 9.

98. *Ibid.*

99. Cutler, D.M. (1994), ''A Guide to Health Care Reform'', *Journal of Economic Perspectives,* Vol. 8, No. 3, p. 18.

100. Victoria has been refining DRGs since 1983.

101. Casemix funding in Australia is also discussed in OECD (1994), *Health Policy Studies,* No. 4, and *Acute Hospital Delivery and Financing* (forthcoming), Paris.

102. The number of patients waiting more than 30 days for urgent surgery fell from 911 on 1 July 1993 to 13 one year later; the number of patients waiting more than 90 days for semi-

urgent treatment dropped by almost half, from 5 569 to 3 095, over the same period; and total waiting lists declined 15 per cent.

103. Aaron, H.J. (1994), p. 34.

104. Pensions were increased by an amount equal to the maximum aggregate out-of-pocket expense so that no pensioner was worse off.

105. "Bulk billing" means that the doctor bills Medicare directly, instead of being paid by patients (who then seek reimbursement from Medicare). To qualify for "bulk billing", the doctor must accept the Medicare rebate (85 per cent of the MBS) as full payment for the service provided.

106. Jackson (1994), p. 6.

107. *Ibid.*

108. An extreme case is arthroscopic knee procedures, which are generally performed on young people and are now almost entirely performed in private hospitals.

109. These are arbitrarily set in public hospitals to gain revenue and are normally lower than in private hospitals. Private insurers thus prefer patients to be treated in public hospitals.

110. Nevertheless, the proportion of the population with private insurance has fallen markedly since Medicare was introduced, from 50 per cent in 1984 to 39.4 per cent in 1993.

111. Indeed, 35 per cent of PBS expenditures is on approximately 12 drugs.

112. This section draws heavily on Jackson (1994).

113. The United States and Belgium are presently experimenting with outpatient casemix – see OECD (1994), *Health Policy Studies,* No. 4, and *Acute Hospital Care Reform* (forthcoming), Paris.

114. If all medical services were not included in the DRG payment, there would be an incentive for care managers to refer patients requiring a lot of follow up to their GPs, shifting costs onto Medicare.

115. This could improve efficiency in public hospitals by 3 to 4 per cent.

Bibliography

Aaron, H.J. (1994), "Issues every plan to reform health care financing must confront", *Journal of economic perspectives,* Vol. 8, No. 3, Summer.

Australian Bureau of Statistics (ABS) (1992), *Deaths Australia,* Catalogue No. 3302, Canberra.

Australian Institute of Health and Welfare (AIHW) (1994), *Australia's Health,* Canberra.

Baume, Peter (1994), "A cutting edge: Australia's surgical workforce", *Report of the Inquiry into the Supply of, and Requirements for, Medical Specialist Services in Australia.*

Blendon, R.J. *et al.* (1990), "Satisfaction with health systems in ten nations", *Health Affairs,* summer.

Bureau of Industry Economics (1994), "International Performance Indicators: Overview", *Research Report 53, AGPS, Canberra.*

Coelli, Michael, Jerome Fahrer and Holly Lindsay (1994), "Wage dispersion and labour market institutions: a cross country study", *Research Discussion Paper No. 9404,* Reserve Bank of Australia, June.

Committee on Employment Opportunities (1993), *Restoring full employment,* A discussion paper, Canberra, December.

Commonwealth of Australia (1994*a*), *Working Nation, Policies and Programs,* Canberra, May.

Commonwealth of Australia (1994*b*), *Working Nation, The White Paper on Employment and Growth,* Canberra, May.

Commonwealth of Australia (1995), *National Fiscal Outlook.*

Commonwealth Treasury (1995), "State and Territory Fiscal Reform", *Economic Roundup,* Summer, pp. 29-38.

Duckett, S.J. and T.J. Jackson (1993), "Casemix classification for outpatient services based on episodes of care", *Medical Journal of Australia,* 158, No. 7, pp. 489-492.

Elliot, Graham, and Ronald Bewley (1994), "The transmission of monetary policy: The relationship between overnight cash rates", *Economic Record,* Vol. 70, March.

Elmeskov, Jorgen (1993), "High and persistent unemployment: Assessment of the problem and its causes", *OECD Economics Department Working Paper,* No. 132.

Fitzgerald, V.W. (1993), *National saving, a report to the Treasurer,* June.

Fraser, B.W. (1994), "The art of monetary policy", *Reserve Bank of Australia Bulletin,* October.

137

Gee, V. (1992), "Perinatal Statistics in Western Australia: ninth annual report of the Western Australian Midwives notification system 1991", *Statistical Series No. 33,* Health Department of Western Australia, Perth.

Gerdtham, Ulf.-G., B. Jönsson, M. MacFarlan and H. Oxley (1995), "Factors affecting health spending: a cross-country econometric analysis", Annex to OECD Working Paper No. 149.

Gillet, S. and L. Mays (1994), *Waiting lists: towards national statistics (an interim report),* Australian Institute of Health and Welfare, Canberra.

Jackson, T.J. (1994), "Resource management: the case for epidose of care payment", Paper presented to "Managing matters in health care 2", The second La Trobe University multidisciplinary conference for health care administrators, 19 August.

Johnson, A. and P. Downes (1994), "The impact of a lower NAIRU on the Australian Macroeconomy: responses to the Treasury Macroeconomic (TRYM) model", Paper presented to the Economic Society of Australia Annual Conference of Economists, September.

Kenyon, Peter (1994), "Restoring full employment: Backing an outsider", *The Australian Economic Review,* 1st quarter.

King, R.G., and S.T. Rebello (1989), "Low frequency filtering and real business cycles", *Rochester University Centre for Economic Research Working Paper,* No. 205, October.

Mays, Larry (1995), *National report on elective surgery waiting lists for public hospitals 1994,* Australian Institute of Health and Welfare.

Mcfarlane, I.J. (1994), "Some recent banking developments", *Reserve Bank of Australia Bulletin,* October.

Mills, Karen, Steven Morling and Waren Tease (1994), "Balance sheet restructuring and investment", *The Australian Economic Review,* 1st quarter.

Murphy, C.W. (1988), "An overview of the Murphy model", *Australian Economic Papers,* Vol. 27, supplement, June.

Northern Territory Department of Health and and Community Services (1992), *The Northern Territory Maternal and Child Health Collection 1991; an analysis of stillbirths, neonatal and infant mortality by ethnicity,* Darwin.

OECD (1987), "Financing and delivering health care: a comparative analysis of seven OECD countries", *Health policy studies No. 2.*

OECD (1993), *Employment Outlook.*

OECD (1993), "OECD health systems: facts and trends", *Health policy studies No. 3.*

OECD (1994), *The OECD Jobs Study,* Facts, Analysis, Strategies.

OECD (1994), *The OECD Jobs Study, Evidence and explanations, Part II: The adjustment potential of the labour market.*

OECD (1994), "Health: quality and choice", *Health policy studies No. 4.*

OECD (forthcoming), "Financing and delivery in acute-care hospitals", *Health policy studies No. 9.*

Orden, David, and Lance A. Fisher (1993), "Financial deregulation and the dynamics of money, prices, and output in New Zealand and Australia", *Journal of Money, Credit, and Banking,* Vol. 25, No. 2, May.

Oxley, H. and M. MacFarlan (1995), "New directions in health-care policy: improving cost control and effectiveness", *Health-care policy series No. 6,* OECD.

Reserve Bank of Australia (1994), "Measuring 'underlying' inflation", *Bulletin,* August.

Sloan, Judith (1994), "An economist's guide to the *Industrial Relations Reform Act*", *IPA Working Paper* No. 1/94, Melbourne, June.

South Australia Health Commission (1993), *Pregnancy outcomes in South Australia 1992,* Pregnancy Outcomes Unit, Epidemiology Branch, South Australia Health Commission.

Stewart, Andrew (1994), "The Industrial Relations Reform Act 1993: Counting the cost", *Australian Bulletin of Labour,* Vol. 20, No. 2, June.

TQA Research Pty Ltd. (1994), *Health care and insurance 1993.*

Victorian Department of Health and Community Services (1993), *Elective surgery activity bulletin,* No. 3, July.

Wooden, Mark, Monica Fan, and Judith Sloan (1994), "The Australian labour market – September 1994", *Australian Bulletin of Labour,* Vol. 20, No. 3, September.

Annex I

Aboriginal health*

Mortality indicators

Death rates of Aboriginals greatly exceed the corresponding Australian rates at all ages (Table A1). The ratio of Aboriginal to Australian age-standardised mortality rates is 2.8 for males and 3.3 for females. The ratio is highest for females aged 25 to 34 years. At 55 to 74 years, the mortality for Aboriginal females is close to that for Aboriginal males whereas in the total population at these ages, female mortality is close to half male mortality.

Although life expectancy for Aboriginals has increased over recent decades, mainly through a reduction in infant mortality, it remains much lower than for the total Australian population. In 1990-92, the average life expectancy at birth of an Aboriginal

Table A1. **Age-specific death rates and ratio by sex, 1990-92**

Per 1 000 population

Age group	Males			Females		
	Aboriginals [1]	Total Australia	Rate ratio	Aboriginals [1]	Total Australia	Rate ratio
0	26.8	8.5	3.2	24.9	6.6	3.8
1-4	1.6	0.4	4.0	1.3	0.3	4.3
5-14	0.5	0.2	2.5	0.5	0.1	5.0
15-24	4.0	1.1	3.6	1.6	0.4	4.0
25-34	6.7	1.3	5.2	3.7	0.5	7.4
35-44	11.2	1.8	6.2	5.8	0.9	6.4
45-54	22.3	4.0	5.6	14.8	2.4	6.2
55-64	36.0	12.3	2.9	35.3	6.5	5.4
65-74	61.9	31.5	2.0	64.0	17.1	3.7
75 and over	138.4	95.3	1.5	103.6	71.9	1.4

1.   Rates for the Aboriginal population are based on data from Western Australia, South Australia and Northern Territory.
Source: Australian Institute of Health and Welfare, unpublished data; Australia Bureau of Statistics (1992).

* This Annex mostly consists of selected extracts from AIHW (1994), pp. 26-36.

Table A2. **Infant and perinatal mortality rates, 1973-91**

Per 1 000 live births

Period	Aboriginals				Total Australia
	Queensland[1]	Western Australia	Southern Australia	Northern Territory	
Infant mortality					
1973-75	78.8	–	–	61.7	15.7
1976-78	56.1	–	–	58.4	12.8
1979-81	27.4	24.7	–	36.8	10.7
1982-84	28.6	24.8	–	32.9	9.7
1985-87	19.3	21.6	20.9	34.9	9.1
1988-90	15.6	22.3	23.2	31.2	8.3
1991	n.a.	19.2[2]	24.9	26.9	7.1
Perinatal mortality					
1973-75	62.6	–	–	53.1	22.3
1976-78	50.8	–	–	60.7	18.2
1979-81	26.8	29.9	–	49.0	14.5
1982-84	29.8	25.6	–	39.3	12.8
1985-87	28.3	19.8	39.8	43.6	11.7
1988-90	26.9	17.6	38.8	44.4	10.8
1991	n.a.	15.6	34.3	32.1	9.6

1. The figures relate to Aboriginals living in the Queensland communities.
2. Estimate provided by the Department of Health, Western Australia.
Source: Northern Territory Department of Health and Community Services (1992), Gee (1992), South Australian Health Commission (1993).

boy was, depending on where he lived, up to 18.2 years shorter than his non-Aboriginal counterpart; and the gap was up to 19.8 years for an Aboriginal girl.

Infant mortality for Aboriginals has fallen dramatically since 1973, partly due to the provision of better health care (Table A2). However, Aboriginal infant mortality remains high, at up to three times the rate for Australians as a whole, depending on location. Perinatal mortality shows similar patterns (see Table A2).

Diseases of the circulatory system, particularly ischaemic heart disease and cerebrovascular disease, and injury and poisoning continue to account for most deaths. The death rate from diseases of the respiratory system was for Aboriginal males 7.3 times that of all Australian males; and for females, the ratio was 7.9. Respiratory infections due to overcrowding, and high rates of smoking, have contributed to these deaths. The other major contributor to excess mortality amongst Aboriginals was diabetes.

Infectious and parasitic diseases also cause disproportionate mortality amongst Aboriginals. Aboriginal mortality from these preventable causes was 12.2 times (males) and 13.4 times (females) that in Australia as a whole in 1990-92.

Measures to improve Aboriginal health

The FY 1994/95 Commonwealth Budget boosted funding for Aboriginal health services by almost A$ 500 million, to be spent over the next five years, extending the Aboriginal Health Strategy until FY 1998/99. Of the A$ 500 million increase in funding, A$ 162 million will be spent on improving the health services available in Aboriginal communities, with the remaining A$ 338 million being spent to improve basic infrastructure, such as clean water, power, housing, sewerage and good nutrition, for the Aboriginal people.

Annex II

Main economic events

1994

January

New road funding arrangements came into effect, confining the Commonwealth's responsibility for the funding of roads to the construction and maintenance of the National Highway System.

February

The report on the regulatory framework within which shipping conferences provide international linear cargo shipping services to and from Australia (the Brazil Report) was released.

The Council of Australian Governments (COAG) agreed the principles of national competition policy articulated in the Hilmer Report (the independent inquiry into national competition policy headed by Professor Fred Hilmer, released on 25 August 1993). The Council agreed that, *inter alia:*

- the Trade Practices Commission and the Prices Surveillance Authority be merged to form the basis for a new national competition body;
- a Working Group of officials be established to develop proposals for implementing the Hilmer recommendations and to report back to the next Council meeting in August 1994.

COAG also endorsed a strategic framework for the efficient and sustainable reform of the Australian water industry, and agreed to its implementation. The framework embraces pricing reform based on the principles of consumption-based pricing and full cost recovery, the reduction or elimination of cross subsidies and making subsidies transparent. It also involves the clarification of property rights, the allocation of water to the environment, the adoption of trading arrangements in water and institutional reform.

March

The Premier's Conference decided that financial assistance grants to the States would be adjusted each year over the period FY 1994/95 to FY 1996/97 for inflation and population growth; this is more beneficial to the States than the guarantee which operated over the preceding three years and was in real terms only. It was also decided to abolish the Loan Council Capital Grants programme, as the distribution of payments under the programme no longer bore any relationship to the States' current infrastructure or fiscal needs.

The Loan Council agreed guidelines for the Loan Council classification of public infrastructure projects with private sector involvement. The guidelines aim to remove Loan Council considerations from governments' decisions about whether to involve the private sector in public infrastructure projects and to increase the transparency of the underlying financial arrangements.

Major provisions of the *Industrial Relations Reform Act* came into effect, including those on enterprise flexibility agreements, which increases the scope for non-unionised and partly-unionised corporations with Federal award coverage to reach agreement directly with employees.

May

The Prime Minister released the White Paper on Employment and Growth known as *Working Nation,* which provided a comprehensive policy response to address high unemployment covering industry policies, employment and regional development.

The Treasurer delivered the FY 1994/95 Budget. It foreshadowed a deficit of A$ 11.7 billion, or 2.5 per cent of GDP, for FY 1994/95 and confirmed and accelerated the fiscal consolidation strategy announced in the FY 1993/94 Budget (which aimed to reduce the Commonwealth budget deficit to around 1 per cent of GDP by FY 1996/97).

The government announced a review of the regulatory and policy issues to be addressed when full and open competition commences in the telecommunications market in July 1997.

As part of the *Working Nation* initiatives, the government introduced a number of measures aimed at encouraging multinational companies to establish regional headquarters (RHQs) in Australia. These measures were: streamlining immigration procedures for RHQ expatriate employees; exempting from dividend withholding tax certain foreign source dividends passed through a resident company to a non-resident shareholder; and permitting RHQs to claim certain relocation expenses as a tax deduction.

June

Agreement between the Federal Labor Government and the Australian Council of Trade Unions was reached regarding continued implementation of the Accord Mark 7 – "Putting Jobs First" – and in particular on the further implementation of safety net adjustments.

The Superannuation Policy Statement was released. The main feature of the Statement was a package of measures addressing the problem of small superannuation account balances being eroded by fees and charges.

The Moomba-Sydney Pipeline was sold to East-Australia Pipeline Limited (owned by AGL Ltd. (51 per cent) and a Canadian-Malaysian consortium (49 per cent)). The sale legislation incorporates a series of provisions to encourage competition in gas transmission.

July

The Job Compact commenced operation.

The Treasurer and Minister for Finance announced the outcome for the FY 1993/94 budget deficit of A$ 13.7 billion, compared with a figure of A$ 16.0 billion forecast in the FY 1993/94 Budget.

August

The National Training Wage was ratified by the Australian Industrial Relations Commission.

The Australian Industrial Relations Commission (AIRC) brought down a decision on the Review of the Wage Fixation Principles emphasising the role of enterprise bargaining as the main avenue for changes in wages and conditions but underpinned by an award safety net.

The Reserve Bank announced an increase of $3/4$ of a percentage point to the official cash rate to around $5^1/2$ per cent. In addition, for capital adequacy requirements, the Bank restricted the 50 per cent weight for housing loans to loans with a loan-to-valuation ratio of 80 per cent or less, with a 100 per cent weight applying to loans with a loan-to-valuation ratio in excess of 80 per cent.

The Council of Australian Governments (COAG) agreed in general to a package of reforms that comprises:

- the revision of the conduct rules of trade practices legislation and their extension to cover State and local government business enterprises and unincorporated businesses;
- the application by individual jurisdictions of agreed principles on structural reform of public monopolies, competitive neutrality between the public and

145

private sectors where they compete, and a programme for the review of regulations restricting competition;

- the establishment in each jurisdiction of a system to carry out surveillance of prices charged by utilities and other corporations with high levels of monopoly power and a regime to provide access to essential facilities such as electricity grids, gas pipelines, airports, rail networks, postal delivery services, communication channels and seaports; and
- the establishment of the Australian Competition Commission (ACC) and the National Competition Council (NCC) to make recommendations in relation to access and pricing surveillance issues and to advise on matters to be determined by governments.

The Council also agreed that all governments should share the benefits of economic growth and revenue from Hilmer and related reforms. An assessment of those benefits is to be prepared by the Industry Commission.

The Government announced reforms to private health insurance arrangements. The reforms will enable insurers to negotiate contracts with individual doctors and hospitals and to market products which for the first time will cover out-of-pocket medical and hospital costs. Complementing this reform will be the development of casemix-episodic payments, which will allow funds to compare hospitals more easily in terms of price and quality, and reforms to strengthen the hand of the consumer.

September

The Commonwealth released the National Competition Policy draft legislative package which contains three elements:

- draft legislation, which amends Part IV of the Trade Practices Act and applies the Act to all persons within State jurisdictions. The legislation also establishes the Australian Competition Commission (ACC), the National Competition Council (NCC) and pricing and access arrangements;
- the draft Intergovernmental Conduct Code Agreement, which includes procedures for extension of the Trade Practices Act and appointments to the ACC; and
- the draft Intergovernmental Competition Principles Agreement, which includes procedures and principles relating to structural reform of public monopolies, legislation review, competitive neutrality, prices oversight and access to essential facilities. It also includes procedures for appointments to the NCC.

Following discussions between the government and the maritime unions, agreement was reached on a package of reforms to improve the performance of the shipping industry.

The Safety Net Adjustment and Review Decision, handed down by the AIRC, provided for three A$ 8 per week safety net wage increase for those workers unable to achieve enterprise agreements. This widened the access to the first safety net adjustment, initially provided by the AIRC in its October 1993 decision, and provided for the second and third adjustments to be available initially at the enterprise level and subsequently at award level over the next two years. The decision also established a process for the review of awards, pursuant to s.150A of the *Industrial Relations Act 1988.*

October

In its response to the Brazil Report, the Government announced that it had agreed to maintain the existing regulatory framework for international liner shipping, together with a few amendments. The Government did not adopt the Report's proposals to establish a Liner Cargo Shipping Authority or to extend regulation to inward trades.

The Australian Government notified the New Zealand Government that it had decided not to allow New Zealand airlines access to the Australian domestic markets from 1 November 1994, nor to grant additional "beyond rights".

The Reserve Bank announced an increase of 1 percentage point in the official cash rate to around 6½ per cent.

November

The AIRC Family Leave Test Case Decision was handed down, allowing employees to have access to their sick leave to care for sick family members, and for employers and employees to agree more flexible leave arrangements, with provision later in 1995 for employees to have access to aggregated sick leave and compassionate leave to look after a sick family member.

December

The *Australian Postal Corporation Amendment Bill 1994* came into law permitting bulk mail customers to interconnect at designated points with Australia Post's network and receive discounts based on the avoidable costs of so doing; the Bill also introduced interconnection for outgoing international mail on the same basis as for domestic mail.

The Reserve Bank announced an increase of 1 percentage point in the official cash rate to around 7½ per cent.

1995

January

The Youth Training Indicative (including revised income support arrangements) came into effect.

The phased introduction of the Australian Vocational Training System commenced.

The Treasurer released on 31 January 1995 the mid-year review of the Budget and the revised economic forecasts for FY 1994/95.

The Treasurer announced details of the mid-year review and the revised economic outlook, and commited the government to tighten fiscal policy structurally in the FY 1995/96 Budget with the intention of bringing the budget into surplus from FY 1996/97, two years earlier than previously anticipated.

STATISTICAL ANNEX AND STRUCTURAL INDICATORS

Table A. **Selected background statistics**

	Average 1984-93	1984	1985	1986	1987	1988	1989	1990	1991	1992	1993
A. Percentage changes from previous year at constant 1989/90 prices											
Private consumption	3.0	3.0	5.1	1.0	2.4	3.9	5.7	2.7	1.0	3.2	2.0
Gross fixed capital formation	2.1	9.9	9.5	-2.8	2.7	8.8	9.1	-7.7	-10.0	-0.6	2.3
Public	2.3	8.4	9.4	8.5	-3.3	-11.8	8.2	1.4	5.0	-2.8	0.3
Private	2.2	10.1	9.5	-4.1	3.5	11.5	9.2	-8.6	-11.7	-0.4	2.6
Residential	4.1	21.2	2.0	-8.7	1.2	22.0	2.6	-12.2	-4.9	8.8	9.6
Non-residential construction	3.2	0.8	24.2	9.5	14.6	18.6	10.8	-9.8	-20.7	-11.0	-4.9
Machinery and equipment	3.0	14.1	11.7	-6.2	2.7	14.9	12.2	-12.3	-11.9	0.3	4.7
Public enterprises	-2.4	-5.4	9.6	-3.3	-0.9	-19.0	15.1	10.5	-12.5	-7.9	-10.2
GDP	3.3	7.5	4.7	2.0	4.7	4.1	4.5	1.3	-1.3	2.1	3.7
GDP price deflator	5.2	6.3	6.2	7.2	7.4	8.4	7.4	4.6	2.0	1.5	1.2
Employment	2.0	2.9	3.6	3.5	2.2	3.8	4.7	1.5	-2.1	-0.7	0.3
Compensation of employees (current prices)	8.0	11.1	9.3	10.9	8.5	11.0	12.6	8.7	1.4	3.4	3.5
Productivity (GDP/employment)	1.3	4.4	1.1	-1.5	2.5	0.3	-0.2	-0.1	0.8	2.8	3.3
Unit labour costs (compensation/GDP)	4.5	3.3	4.4	8.7	3.6	6.6	7.7	7.3	2.7	1.3	-0.2
B. Percentage ratios											
Gross fixed capital formation as % of GDP at constant prices	22.9	23.6	24.7	23.6	23.1	24.2	25.2	23.0	21.0	20.4	20.1
Stockbuilding as % of GDP at constant prices	0.3	1.1	0.5	-0.2	-0.2	0.6	1.4	0.3	-0.7	-0.2	0.3
Foreign balance as % of GDP at constant prices	0.2	-1.8	-1.0	0.4	1.9	-0.0	-2.6	-0.6	2.1	1.7	2.1
Compensation of employees as % of GDP at current prices	50.2	51.6	50.7	51.4	49.6	48.8	48.9	50.2	50.6	50.5	49.8
Direct taxes as per cent of household income	21.6	21.8	21.3	22.6	24.1	23.9	23.0	21.2	20.3	19.0	19.3
Unemployment as per cent of total labour force	8.4	8.9	8.1	8.0	8.0	7.1	6.1	7.0	9.5	10.7	10.9
C. Other indicator											
Current balance (US$ billion)	-10.7	-8.6	-8.7	-9.2	-7.4	-10.0	-17.4	-14.8	-9.8	-10.6	-10.4

Source: Australian Bureau of Statistics and OECD Secretariat.

Table B. Gross domestic product

A$ million

	1984	1985	1986	1987	1988	1989	1990	1991	1992	1993
	Current prices									
Private consumption[1]	121 862	136 858	150 003	165 795	184 206	207 513	225 945	236 345	248 194	257 909
Government current expenditure[1]	38 207	42 446	47 326	50 363	54 558	59 112	65 004	69 598	72 734	75 394
Gross fixed capital formation[2]	47 188	56 376	61 044	67 279	77 639	90 255	86 117	78 096	77 649	81 080
Private	32 890	39 444	42 555	48 331	61 024	70 478	64 333	57 249	57 995	62 550
Public enterprises	8 650	10 311	10 756	11 120	9 435	11 613	13 228	11 768	10 854	9 642
Government	5 648	6 621	7 733	7 828	7 180	8 164	8 556	9 079	8 800	8 888
Change in stocks	2 098	1 189	−750	−11	1 970	4 975	433	−2 524	−507	907
Exports of goods and services	31 437	38 708	40 763	47 600	53 573	58 428	63 825	68 392	73 321	79 659
Imports of goods and services	35 624	44 238	47 189	50 027	56 416	67 074	67 186	66 363	73 957	81 348
Statistical discrepancy	1 089	−1 964	−365	953	2 632	3 831	4 326	−2 703	−3 101	231
Gross domestic product at purchasers' values[3]	206 257	229 375	250 832	281 952	318 162	357 040	378 464	380 841	394 333	413 832
Indirect taxes less subsidies	24 077	28 239	29 187	34 952	38 980	42 777	44 838	44 630	44 846	47 850
Gross domestic product at factor cost	182 179	201 135	221 644	246 999	279 181	314 262	333 625	336 210	349 486	365 981
	Average 1989/90 prices									
Private consumption[1]	179 229	188 314	190 233	194 776	202 342	213 921	219 723	221 859	229 006	233 572
Government current expenditure[1]	50 653	53 249	55 758	56 920	58 876	60 261	63 124	64 825	65 772	66 658
Gross fixed capital formation[2]	71 168	77 950	75 781	77 826	84 709	92 386	85 291	76 735	76 242	78 010
Private	51 462	56 366	53 927	56 386	66 719	72 211	63 762	56 415	57 075	59 892
Public enterprises	12 080	13 240	12 804	12 685	10 272	11 826	13 064	11 429	10 525	9 452
Government	7 626	8 344	9 050	8 755	7 718	8 349	8 465	8 891	8 642	8 666
Change in stocks	3 165	1 666	−745	−589	2 048	5 117	931	−2 483	−706	1 149
Exports of goods and services	42 764	47 311	49 546	55 418	57 156	59 170	63 961	72 185	75 869	81 168
Imports of goods and services	48 218	50 433	48 126	49 008	57 180	68 799	66 264	64 645	69 586	73 157
Statistical discrepancy	2 242	−2 824	−932	1 253	2 442	4 151	4 240	−2 308	−2 918	135
Gross domestic product at purchasers' values[3]	301 003	315 233	321 515	336 596	350 393	366 207	371 006	366 168	373 679	387 535

1. Not adjusted for the impact of the introduction of Medicare from 1 February 1986, which had the effect of transferring certain expenditures on healthcare, formerly included as private consumption expenditure, to public consumption expenditure.
2. Not adjusted to remove the impact of the sale of public sector assets under leaseback and similar arrangements.
3. Income-based measure.
Source: Australian Bureau of Statistics.

Table C.   **Income and expenditure of households (including unincorporated enterprises)**

A$ million, current prices

	1984	1985	1986	1987	1988	1989	1990	1991	1992	1993
Compensation of employees	106 465	116 398	128 959	139 917	154 814	174 960	190 364	192 806	198 283	206 447
Income from property and entrepreneurship	34 992	38 856	44 016	50 319	58 162	66 990	69 990	65 873	64 342	63 832
Farm	2 832	2 379	1 463	2 658	4 740	3 831	2 434	1 081	2 732	2 898
Non-farm	32 160	36 477	42 553	47 661	53 422	63 159	67 556	64 792	61 610	60 934
Current transfers from government	20 177	22 094	23 983	26 318	28 508	30 786	34 701	39 878	44 394	47 572
Grants to non-profit institutions	2 561	2 878	3 192	3 249	3 759	4 106	4 771	5 256	5 849	6 589
Third party insurance transfers	1 349	1 497	1 499	1 512	1 538	1 664	1 673	1 626	1 639	1 696
Unrequited transfers from overseas	1 234	1 689	1982	2 480	2 972	3 553	3 429	3 632	3 054	2 047
Income	166 778	183 412	203 631	223 795	249 753	282 059	304 928	309 071	317 561	328 183
less: Income taxes	27 327	30 146	35 181	40 671	44 756	48 669	49 789	48 545	47 076	49 045
of which: Direct taxes paid on income	1 270	1 333	1 484	1 717	1 977	2 255	2 498	2 661	2 834	3 035
Consumer debt interest	2 501	3 159	4 133	4 532	4 920	7 256	7 712	6 275	4 482	3 705
Transfers paid by households	699	692	749	765	798	875	960	1 002	1 020	1 000
Disposable income	134 981	148 082	162 084	176 110	197 302	223 004	243 969	250 588	262 149	271 398
Consumption expenditure	121 862	136 858	150 003	165 795	184 206	207 513	225 945	236 345	248 194	257 909
Saving	13 119	11 224	12 081	10 315	13 096	15 491	18 024	14 243	13 955	13 489
as per cent of disposable income	9.7	7.6	7.5	5.9	6.6	6.9	7.4	5.7	5.3	5.0

Source: Australian Bureau of Statistics.

Table D. **Prices and wages**

	1984	1985	1986	1987	1988	1989	1990	1991	1992	1993
						Index FY 1989/90 = 100				
Price deflators										
Gross domestic product	68.5	72.7	78.0	83.7	90.8	97.5	102.0	104.0	105.5	106.8
Private consumption	68.0	72.7	78.8	85.1	91.0	97.0	102.8	106.5	108.4	110.4
Gross fixed capital formation	66.3	72.3	80.5	86.4	91.6	97.7	100.9	101.7	101.8	103.9
Exports[1]	73.5	81.8	82.2	85.9	93.8	98.7	99.8	94.8	96.7	98.2
Imports[1]	73.8	87.6	98.1	102.0	98.9	97.4	101.4	102.7	106.2	111.1
Terms of trade[1]	99.6	93.6	83.9	84.1	95.0	101.4	98.5	92.4	91.1	88.4
Consumer price index[2]										
Total	66.0	70.5	76.8	83.3	89.4	96.2	103.2	106.5	107.6	109.5
Food	63.3	65.6	70.1	76.5	83.5	89.5	96.0	103.6	106.9	107.9
Award rates of pay, adult persons	76.0	78.8	83.1	86.5	91.4	97.0	103.0	106.9	109.5	110.5
Average weekly earnings, all employees	72.0	75.4	80.7	84.9	90.6	96.9	103.3	107.2	109.9	113.0

1. Goods and services.
2. Not adjusted for the effects of Medicare.
Source: Australian Bureau of Statistics, Reserve Bank, and OECD Secretariat.

Table E. **Balance of payments**

OECD basis, US$ million

	1984	1985	1986	1987	1988	1989	1990	1991	1992	1993
Exports, fob	22 862	22 654	22 430	26 955	33 043	36 912	39 281	41 993	42 395	42 179
Imports, fob	23 685	23 633	24 258	26 698	33 650	40 361	38 905	38 475	40 875	42 327
Trade balance	-823	-979	-1 828	257	-606	-3 449	376	3 518	1 520	-148
Invisibles, net	-7 837	-7 735	-7 469	-7 784	-9 597	-14 262	-15 459	-13 789	-12 480	-10 627
Current balance	-8 661	-8 714	-9 297	-7 527	-10 204	-17 711	-15 083	-10 271	-10 960	-10 775
Long-term capital (excluding special transactions)	6 617	7 590	10 066	8 888	18 890	14 967	11 999	12 216	9 733	9 081
Private	5 908	6 299	8 195	7 360	19 484	14 008	12 266	10 851	4 257	1 232
Official	709	1 291	1 872	1 528	-595	959	-267	1 364	5 476	7 849
Basic balance	-2 044	-1 124	769	1 361	8 686	-2 744	-3 085	1 946	-1 227	-1 693
Non-monetary short-term capital	-443	-613	119	-621	-6	-892	-364	1 194	583	376
Errors and omissions	1 269	-417	656	-563	-3 700	2 540	5 391	-3 658	-3 641	1 361
Balance on non-monetary transactions	-1 218	-2 154	1 545	177	4 980	-1 097	1 942	-517	-4 285	44
Private monetary institutions' short-term capital	-27	-141	-871	85	339	1 735	-194	198	-410	-53
a) Assets	-49	-219	-635	-380	-203	-131	-841	886	-771	-931
b) Liabilities	22	78	-236	465	542	1 866	647	-688	361	878
Balance on official settlements	-1 245	-2 295	674	262	5 320	638	1 748	-319	-4 694	-10
Use of IMF credit	–	–	–	–	–	–	–	–	–	–
Special transactions	–	–	–	–	–	–	–	–	–	–
Miscellaneous official accounts	1	–	–	–	–	–	-1	–	–	-19
Allocations of SDRs	–	–	–	–	–	–	–	–	–	–
Change in reserves (+ = increase)	-1 244	-2 295	674	262	5 320	638	1 747	-319	-4 694	-29
a) Gold	–	–	–	–	–	–	–	–	–	-13
b) Current assets	-1 463	-2 366	687	277	5 316	603	1 769	-297	-4 757	24
c) Reserve position in IMF	80	2	–	–	20	53	–	–	258	-26
d) Special Drawing Rights	139	69	-13	-15	-16	-18	-22	-22	-195	-14

Source: Balance-of-payments submission to OECD.

Table F. Foreign trade by commodity

SITC sections:	US$ million					Per cent of total				
	1980	1985	1990	1992	1993	1980	1985	1990	1992	1993
Total exports, fob	21 309	21 899	35 626	38 047	37 843	100.0	100.0	100.0	100.0	100.0
Food and live animals	7 171	5 227	6 802	5 864	5 906	33.7	23.9	19.1	15.4	15.6
Beverages and tobacco	48	45	155	221	274	0.2	0.2	0.4	0.6	0.7
Crude materials, inedible, except fuels	6 116	6 281	6 657	7 043	5 880	28.7	28.7	18.7	18.5	15.5
Mineral fuels, lubricants and related materials	2 363	5 853	6 656	7 673	7 453	11.1	26.7	18.7	20.2	19.7
Animals and vegetable oils, fats and waxes	114	95	45	81	128	0.5	0.4	0.1	0.2	0.3
Chemicals and related products, n.e.s.	475	368	830	1 105	1 229	2.2	1.7	2.3	2.9	3.2
Manufactured goods classified chiefly by material	2 483	2 224	4 408	4 824	4 669	11.7	10.2	12.4	12.7	12.3
Machinery and transport equipment	1 149	751	2 258	2 992	3 477	5.4	3.4	6.3	7.9	9.2
Miscellaneous manufactured articles	378	346	775	898	972	1.8	1.6	2.2	2.4	2.6
Commodities and transactions not classified according to kind	1 012	709	7 040	7 346	7 855	4.7	3.2	19.8	18.6	18.6
Total imports, cif	19 863	23 738	38 462	42 140	43 454	100.0	100.0	100.0	100.0	100.0
Food and live animals	760	939	1 459	1 564	1 618	3.8	4.0	3.8	3.7	3.7
Beverages and tobacco	182	189	313	304	308	0.9	0.8	0.8	0.7	0.7
Crude materials, inedible, except fuels	865	689	1 068	1 014	1 024	4.4	2.9	2.8	2.4	2.4
Mineral fuels, lubricants and related materials	2 749	1 592	2 192	2 392	2 570	13.8	6.7	5.7	5.7	5.9
Animals and vegetable oils, fats and waxes	79	75	97	127	128	0.4	0.3	0.3	0.3	0.3
Chemicals and related products, n.e.s.	1 784	1 994	3 497	3 964	4 112	9.0	8.4	9.1	9.4	9.5
Manufactured goods classified chiefly by material	3 528	3 773	5 870	6 136	6 133	17.8	15.9	15.3	14.6	14.1
Machinery and transport equipment	7 211	9 885	17 192	17 001	18 308	36.3	41.6	44.7	40.3	42.1
Miscellaneous manufactured articles	2 426	3 095	5 320	6 141	6 270	12.2	13.0	13.8	14.6	14.4
Commodities and transactions not classified according to kind	278	1 506	1 454	3 497	2 983	1.4	6.3	3.8	8.3	6.9

Source: OECD, *Foreign Trade Statistics*, Series C.

155

Table G. **Foreign trade by area**
US$ million

	1984	1985	1986	1987	1988	1989	1990	1991	1992	1993
Exports, fob										
OECD Europe	3 523	3 321	3 643	4 776	5 272	5 814	6 241	5 951	6 196	5 510
of which: United Kingdom	891	777	818	1 139	1 166	1 323	1 399	1 330	1 664	1 911
OECD North America	2 905	2 596	2 760	3 435	4 088	4 439	4 921	4 835	4 406	4 235
Japan	6 139	6 304	6 065	6 789	8 882	9 761	10 205	11 537	10 713	10 441
New Zealand	1 409	1 063	1 032	1 511	1 629	1 891	1 956	2 043	2 241	2 466
Far East	5 190	5 092	5 125	6 273	8 468	9 830	10 677	13 068	14 582	14 948
Other non-OECD countries	4 054	3 723	3 531	3 316	3 864	4 491	3 951	3 656	3 463	3 735
Non-specified	637	515	381	404	463	762	956	841	835	1 058
Total	23 861	22 617	22 541	26 508	32 670	36 991	38 911	41 934	42 439	42 392
Imports, cif										
OECD Europe	5 947	6 281	6 877	7 713	9 407	10 835	10 630	9 600	9 945	9 996
of which: United Kingdom	1 627	1 653	1 792	1 950	2 467	2 785	2 701	2 400	2 412	2 410
OECD North America	5 599	5 723	5 714	6 342	7 986	10 242	10 234	10 113	9 930	9 828
Japan	5 116	5 432	5 348	5 321	6 713	8 319	7 307	6 807	7 373	8 073
New Zealand	875	956	918	1 109	1 462	1 661	1 715	1 768	1 876	2 065
Far East	3 638	3 333	3 572	4 806	5 935	7 299	6 706	7 733	8 738	9 213
Other non-OECD countries	2 131	1 731	1 461	1 685	1 778	2 497	2 480	2 629	2 825	3 176
Non-specified	116	51	25	32	55	91	62	70	66	71
Total	23 424	23 511	23 919	27 010	33 339	40 948	39 138	38 723	40 755	42 422

Source: OECD, *Foreign Trade Statistics*, Series A.

156

Table H. Production structure and performance indicators

Fiscal years[1]

	1975	1980	1985	1990	1992	1975	1980	1985	1990	1992
	GDP share					Employment share				
A. Production structure (constant prices)										
Tradeables										
Agriculture	5.1	4.0	4.4	4.4	4.3	6.8	6.6	6.2	5.6	5.3
Mining and quarrying	3.9	3.7	4.4	4.6	4.6	1.4	1.4	1.5	1.2	1.1
Manufacturing	19.2	18.6	16.4	15.3	15.0	21.6	19.7	16.7	15.0	14.5
Non-tradeables										
Electricity, gas and water	2.7	3.0	3.2	3.3	3.3	1.8	2.1	2.1	1.3	1.3
Construction	9.1	9.0	8.2	7.5	6.7	8.7	7.7	6.9	7.3	7.0
Trade, restaurants and hotels	19.7	18.8	17.8	17.0	17.1	19.8	20.1	22.9	24.3	24.7
Transport, storage and communication	5.3	6.3	6.6	7.2	7.6	7.8	7.4	7.6	7.0	6.4
Finance, insurance, real estate and business services	18.9	20.2	21.1	22.2	22.0	7.4	8.5	10.1	11.5	11.4
Community, social and personal services	14.5	14.6	15.3	16.0	16.5	19.9	22.1	21.2	22.1	23.5
	Productivity growth[2]					Investment share				
B. Economic performance (constant prices)										
Agriculture	–	–2.3	4.4	–0.5	6.6	9.0	10.4	8.4	6.0	5.6
Mining and quarrying	–	–0.5	2.8	5.8	5.7	6.9	6.3	6.7	7.2	9.4
Manufacturing	–	2.8	2.1	1.8	4.0	15.3	13.8	12.0	15.0	14.2
Electricity, gas and water	–	0.8	2.3	10.8	11.7	12.2	13.6	11.2	6.6	8.4
Construction	–	3.8	1.7	–2.5	1.3	2.8	3.4	4.2	2.8	2.0
Trade, restaurants and hotels	–	0.3	–2.3	–0.3	2.0	8.7	8.6	9.8	9.9	10.4
Transport, storage and communication	–	5.9	2.1	5.3	13.6	14.9	13.0	13.8	15.2	15.8
Finance, insurance, real estate and business services	–	0.0	–1.2	–0.6	5.0	10.5	9.5	12.7	18.6	12.2
Community, social and personal services	–	–0.3	3.0	1.1	3.1	1.7	2.5	2.0	2.7	2.3
	1980	1985	1986	1987	1988	1989	1990	1991	1992	1993
C. Other indicators (current prices)										
Effective rate of protection, manufacturing	22	20	19	19	17	16	14	13	12	10
R&D in manufacturing/ manufacturing GDP	..	1.8	1.6	1.7	1.8	1.8	1.9	2.2	..	
Levels of net foreign debt[3]/GDP	5.6	23.7	31.6	32.6	32.2	34.3	35.7	37.6	39.6	41.8
Levels of foreign direct investment[3]/ GDP	17.1	17.0	17.0	20.8	22.1	24.6	25.4	26.1	27.1	29.5

1. Beginning 1st July of the year indicated.
2. Average rate of growth between periods.
3. At 30th June of the year indicated.

Source: Australian Bureau of Statistics, International Investment Position Australia; Industry Assistance Commission, Annual Report 1990-91; OECD, *Main Science and Technology Indicators* and *National Accounts*.

Table I. **Labour market indicators**

	A. Evolution					
	Peak	Trough	1985	1990	1992	1993
Standardised unemployment rate	1993: 10.8	1981: 5.7	8.2	6.9	10.7	10.8
Unemployment rate						
Total	1993: 10.8	1981: 5.7	8.2	6.9	10.7	10.8
Male	1993: 11.4	1981: 4.7	7.8	6.7	11.2	11.4
Female	1983: 10.4	1990: 7.2	8.8	7.2	10.0	10.1
Youth [1]	1992: 19.5	1989: 10.4	14.3	13.3	19.5	18.6
Share of long-term unemployment [2]	1993: 36.5	1982: 19.0	30.9	21.6	34.5	36.5
Non-farm vacancies (thousand)	1989: 68.2	1983: 17.6	54.0	48.3	27.2	34.3
Average hours worked in						
manufacturing, weekly	1970: 39.5	1983: 35.6	37.0	38.2	37.6	38.0
Overtime hours per week, non-farm	1989: 1.5	1984: 1.1	1.2	1.3	1.1	1.2

	B. Structural or institutional characteristics					
	1970	1980	1985	1990	1992	1993
Labour force (percentage change) [3]	..	2.0	1.8	2.9	0.6	0.6
Participation rate [4]						
Total	61.2	61.0	60.2	63.8	63.0	62.6
Male	83.0	77.9	75.2	75.7	74.3	73.7
Female	39.6	44.7	45.7	52.2	51.9	51.8
Employment by sector						
Per cent of total						
Agriculture	8.0	6.5	6.1	5.6	5.3	5.3
Industry	37.0	31.0	27.6	25.4	23.8	23.8
Services	55.0	62.5	66.2	69.1	70.9	70.8
Percentage change [3]						
Agriculture	..	–0.6	0.4	1.2	–3.6	1.1
Industry	..	–0.1	–1.2	1.5	–1.5	0.4
Services	..	2.8	2.4	4.2	–0.1	0.4
Total	..	1.5	1.2	3.2	–0.5	0.4
Part-time employment						
(per cent of total employed)	10.6	16.4	18.2	21.3	24.4	23.5
Non-wage labour cost [5]	3.0	5.6	7.5	7.6	8.6	9.5

1. People between 15 and 24 years as a percentage of the labour force of the same age group.
2. People looking for a job for one year or more as a percentage of total unemployment.
3. Average rate of growth between periods.
4. Labour force as a percentage of the corresponding population aged between 15 and 64 years.
5. Total social contributions as a percentage of total compensation.
Source: Australian Bureau of Statistics; OECD, *Labour Force Statistics.*

Table J. **The public sector**

	1973	1980	1985	1990	1992	1993
Budget indicators: General government accounts (per cent of GDP)						
Current receipts (excluding interests)	24.0	28.1	30.7	31.7	29.8	29.8
Non-interest expenditures	23.9	29.3	32.3	29.8	33.2	33.4
Primary budget balance	0.2	−1.2	−1.7	1.9	−3.4	−3.6
Net interest (including net capital transfers)	−0.1	−0.4	−1.1	−1.4	−0.5	−0.1
General government budget balance	0.1	−1.5	−2.7	0.5	−3.9	−3.7
Structure of expenditure and taxation (per cent of GDP)						
Government expenditure	24.0	30.9	35.3	33.7	36.8	36.7
Transfers	6.9	9.6	11.2	10.8	12.9	13.2
Subsidies	1.1	1.5	1.8	1.3	1.5	1.6
General expenditure [1]						
Education	3.6	4.5	4.3	3.7	3.9	..
Transportation	1.5	1.6	1.6	1.5	1.5	..
Health	2.0	3.1	3.2	3.2	3.1	..
Tax receipts [1]	25.3	28.5	30.0	30.8	29.6	28.9
Personal income tax	10.3	12.5	13.6	13.2	11.7	11.8
Corporate tax	3.8	3.5	2.8	4.4	4.1	3.7
Payroll tax	1.3	1.4	1.4	1.9	1.8	1.8
Taxes on goods and services	7.5	8.8	9.9	8.6	8.1	8.6
of which: Specific taxes on consumption	4.7	6.4	6.2	4.7	4.2	4.4
Other indicators						
Income tax elasticity [1]	1.7 [2]	1.2	1.1	0.1	0.4	1.3
Income tax as a percentage of total tax [1]	40.5	44.0	45.3	43.0	40.9	40.8
Net public debt as a percentage of GDP	..	..	..	11.6	15.3	19.7

	Prior to		After
Tax rates (per cent)			
Top rate of income tax	49	1st January 1990	47
Lower rate of income tax	21	1st January 1991	20
Corporation tax rate	39	1st July 1993	33

1.   Fiscal years beginning 1st July.
2.   1974 figure.
Source: Australian Bureau of Statistics; OECD, *National Accounts, Revenue Statistics of OECD Member countries* and Secretariat estimates.

BASIC STATISTICS:

INTERNATIONAL COMPARISONS

	Units	Reference period [1]	Australia	Austria
Population				
Total	Thousands	1992	17 489	7 884
Inhabitants per sq. km	Number	1992	2	94
Net average annual increase over previous 10 years	%	1992	1.4	0.4
Employment				
Civilian employment (CE) [2]	Thousands	1992	7 637	3 546
Of which: Agriculture	% of CE		5.3	7.1
Industry	% of CE		23.8	35.6
Services	% of CE		71	57.4
Gross domestic product (GDP)				
At current prices and current exchange rates	Bill. US$	1992	296.6	186.2
Per capita	US$		16 959	23 616
At current prices using current PPPs [3]	Bill. US$	1992	294.5	142
Per capita	US$		16 800	18 017
Average annual volume growth over previous 5 years	%	1992	2	3.4
Gross fixed capital formation (GFCF)	% of GDP	1992	19.7	25
Of which: Machinery and equipment	% of GDP		9.3	9.9
Residential construction.	% of GDP		5.1	5.7
Average annual volume growth over previous 5 years	%	1992	−1	5.1
Gross saving ratio [4]	% of GDP	1992	15.6	25.1
General government				
Current expenditure on goods and services	% of GDP	1992	18.5	18.4
Current disbursements [5]	% of GDP	1992	36.9	46.2
Current receipts	% of GDP	1992	33.1	48.3
Net official development assistance	% of GNP	1992	0.33	0.3
Indicators of living standards				
Private consumption per capita using current PPPs [3]	US$	1992	10 527	9 951
Passenger cars, per 1 000 inhabitants	Number	1990	430	382
Telephones, per 1 000 inhabitants	Number	1990	448	589
Television sets, per 1 000 inhabitants	Number	1989	484	475
Doctors, per 1 000 inhabitants	Number	1991	2	2.1
Infant mortality per 1 000 live births	Number	1991	7.1	7.4
Wages and prices (average annual increase over previous 5 years)				
Wages (earnings or rates according to availability)	%	1992	5	5.4
Consumer prices	%	1992	5.2	3
Foreign trade				
Exports of goods, fob*	Mill. US$	1992	42 844	44 361
As % of GDP	%		14.4	23.8
Average annual increase over previous 5 years	%		10.1	10.4
Imports of goods, cif*	Mill. US$	1992	40 751	54 038
As % of GDP	%		13.7	29
Average annual increase over previous 5 years	%		8.6	10.7
Total official reserves [6]	Mill. SDRs	1992	8 152	9 006
As ratio of average monthly imports of goods	Ratio		2.4	2

* At current prices and exchange rates.
1. Unless otherwise stated.
2. According to the definitions used in OECD *Labour Force Statistics.*
3. PPPs = Purchasing Power Parities.
4. Gross saving = Gross national disposable income minus private and government consumption.
5. Current disbursements = Current expenditure on goods and services plus current transfers and payments of property income.
6. Gold included in reserves is valued at 35 SDRs per ounce. End of year.
7. Including Luxembourg.

EMPLOYMENT OPPORTUNITIES

Economics Department, OECD

The Economics Department of the OECD offers challenging and rewarding opportunities to economists interested in applied policy analysis in an international environment. The Department's concerns extend across the entire field of economic policy analysis, both macroeconomic and microeconomic. Its main task is to provide, for discussion by committees of senior officials from Member countries, documents and papers dealing with current policy concerns. Within this programme of work, three major responsibilities are:

- to prepare regular surveys of the economies of individual Member countries;
- to issue full twice-yearly reviews of the economic situation and prospects of the OECD countries in the context of world economic trends;
- to analyse specific policy issues in a medium-term context for the OECD as a whole, and to a lesser extent for the non-OECD countries.

The documents prepared for these purposes, together with much of the Department's other economic work, appear in published form in the *OECD Economic Outlook, OECD Economic Surveys, OECD Economic Studies* and the Department's *Working Papers* series.

The Department maintains a world econometric model, INTERLINK, which plays an important role in the preparation of the policy analyses and twice-yearly projections. The availability of extensive cross-country data bases and good computer resources facilitates comparative empirical analysis, much of which is incorporated into the model.

The Department is made up of about 80 professional economists from a variety of backgrounds and Member countries. Most projects are carried out by small teams and last from four to eighteen months. Within the Department, ideas and points of view are widely discussed; there is a lively professional interchange, and all professional staff have the opportunity to contribute actively to the programme of work.

Skills the Economics Department is looking for:

a) Solid competence in using the tools of both microeconomic and macroeconomic theory to answer policy questions. Experience indicates that this normally requires the equivalent of a Ph.D. in economics or substantial relevant professional experience to compensate for a lower degree.

b) Solid knowledge of economic statistics and quantitative methods; this includes how to identify data, estimate structural relationships, apply basic techniques of time series analysis, and test hypotheses. It is essential to be able to interpret results sensibly in an economic policy context.

c) A keen interest in and extensive knowledge of policy issues, economic developments and their political/social contexts.

d) Interest and experience in analysing questions posed by policy-makers and presenting the results to them effectively and judiciously. Thus, work experience in government agencies or policy research institutions is an advantage.

e) The ability to write clearly, effectively, and to the point. The OECD is a bilingual organisation with French and English as the official languages. Candidates must have excellent knowledge of one of these languages, and some knowledge of the other. Knowledge of other languages might also be an advantage for certain posts.

f) For some posts, expertise in a particular area may be important, but a successful candidate is expected to be able to work on a broader range of topics relevant to the work of the Department. Thus, except in rare cases, the Department does not recruit narrow specialists.

g) The Department works on a tight time schedule with strict deadlines. Moreover, much of the work in the Department is carried out in small groups. Thus, the ability to work with other economists from a variety of cultural and professional backgrounds, to supervise junior staff, and to produce work on time is important.

General information

The salary for recruits depends on educational and professional background. Positions carry a basic salary from FF 305 700 or FF 377 208 for Administrators (economists) and from FF 438 348 for Principal Administrators (senior economists). This may be supplemented by expatriation and/or family allowances, depending on nationality, residence and family situation. Initial appointments are for a fixed term of two to three years.

Vacancies are open to candidates from OECD Member countries. The Organisation seeks to maintain an appropriate balance between female and male staff and among nationals from Member countries.

For further information on employment opportunities in the Economics Department, contact:

Administrative Unit
Economics Department
OECD
2, rue André-Pascal
75775 PARIS CEDEX 16
FRANCE

E-Mail: compte.esadmin@oecd.org

Applications citing ''ECSUR'', together with a detailed *curriculum vitae* in English or French, should be sent to the Head of Personnel at the above address.

MAIN SALES OUTLETS OF OECD PUBLICATIONS
PRINCIPAUX POINTS DE VENTE DES PUBLICATIONS DE L'OCDE

ARGENTINA – ARGENTINE
Carlos Hirsch S.R.L.
Galería Güemes, Florida 165, 4° Piso
1333 Buenos Aires   Tel. (1) 331.1787 y 331.2391
Telefax: (1) 331.1787

AUSTRALIA – AUSTRALIE
D.A. Information Services
648 Whitehorse Road, P.O.B 163
Mitcham, Victoria 3132   Tel. (03) 873.4411
Telefax: (03) 873.5679

AUSTRIA – AUTRICHE
Gerold & Co.
Graben 31
Wien I   Tel. (0222) 533.50.14

BELGIUM – BELGIQUE
Jean De Lannoy
Avenue du Roi 202
B-1060 Bruxelles   Tel. (02) 538.51.69/538.08.41
Telefax: (02) 538.08.41

CANADA
Renouf Publishing Company Ltd.
1294 Algoma Road
Ottawa, ON K1B 3W8   Tel. (613) 741.4333
Telefax: (613) 741.5439
Stores:
61 Sparks Street
Ottawa, ON K1P 5R1   Tel. (613) 238.8985
211 Yonge Street
Toronto, ON M5B 1M4   Tel. (416) 363.3171
Telefax: (416)363.59.63
Les Éditions La Liberté Inc.
3020 Chemin Sainte-Foy
Sainte-Foy, PQ G1X 3V6   Tel. (418) 658.3763
Telefax: (418) 658.3763

Federal Publications Inc.
165 University Avenue, Suite 701
Toronto, ON M5H 3B8   Tel. (416) 860.1611
Telefax: (416) 860.1608
Les Publications Fédérales
1185 Université
Montréal, QC H3B 3A7   Tel. (514) 954.1633
Telefax : (514) 954.1635

CHINA – CHINE
China National Publications Import
Export Corporation (CNPIEC)
16 Gongti E. Road, Chaoyang District
P.O. Box 88 or 50
Beijing 100704 PR   Tel. (01) 506.6688
Telefax: (01) 506.3101

CZECH REPUBLIC – RÉPUBLIQUE TCHÈQUE
Artia Pegas Press Ltd.
Narodni Trida 25
POB 825
111 21 Praha 1   Tel. 26.65.68
Telefax: 26.20.81

DENMARK – DANEMARK
Munksgaard Book and Subscription Service
35, Nørre Søgade, P.O. Box 2148
DK-1016 København K   Tel. (33) 12.85.70
Telefax: (33) 12.93.87

EGYPT – ÉGYPTE
Middle East Observer
41 Sherif Street
Cairo   Tel. 392.6919
Telefax: 360-6804

FINLAND – FINLANDE
Akateeminen Kirjakauppa
Keskuskatu 1, P.O. Box 128
00100 Helsinki
Subscription Services/Agence d'abonnements :
P.O. Box 23
00371 Helsinki   Tel. (358 0) 12141
Telefax: (358 0) 121.4450

FRANCE
OECD/OCDE
Mail Orders/Commandes par correspondance:
2, rue André-Pascal
75775 Paris Cedex 16   Tel. (33-1) 45.24.82.00
Telefax: (33-1) 49.10.42.76
Telex: 640048 OCDE
Orders via Minitel, France only/
Commandes par Minitel, France exclusivement :
36 15 OCDE

OECD Bookshop/Librairie de l'OCDE :
33, rue Octave-Feuillet
75016 Paris   Tel. (33-1) 45.24.81.67
(33-1) 45.24.81.81

Documentation Française
29, quai Voltaire
75007 Paris   Tel. 40.15.70.00

Gibert Jeune (Droit-Économie)
6, place Saint-Michel
75006 Paris   Tel. 43.25.91.19

Librairie du Commerce International
10, avenue d'Iéna
75016 Paris   Tel. 40.73.34.60

Librairie Dunod
Université Paris-Dauphine
Place du Maréchal de Lattre de Tassigny
75016 Paris   Tel. (1) 44.05.40.13

Librairie Lavoisier
11, rue Lavoisier
75008 Paris   Tel. 42.65.39.95

Librairie L.G.D.J. - Montchrestien
20, rue Soufflot
75005 Paris   Tel. 46.33.89.85

Librairie des Sciences Politiques
30, rue Saint-Guillaume
75007 Paris   Tel. 45.48.36.02

P.U.F.
49, boulevard Saint-Michel
75005 Paris   Tel. 43.25.83.40

Librairie de l'Université
12a, rue Nazareth
13100 Aix-en-Provence   Tel. (16) 42.26.18.08

Documentation Française
165, rue Garibaldi
69003 Lyon   Tel. (16) 78.63.32.23

Librairie Decitre
29, place Bellecour
69002 Lyon   Tel. (16) 72.40.54.54

GERMANY – ALLEMAGNE
OECD Publications and Information Centre
August-Bebel-Allee 6
D-53175 Bonn   Tel. (0228) 959.120
Telefax: (0228) 959.12.17

GREECE – GRÈCE
Librairie Kauffmann
Mavrokordatou 9
106 78 Athens   Tel. (01) 32.55.321
Telefax: (01) 36.33.967

HONG-KONG
Swindon Book Co. Ltd.
13–15 Lock Road
Kowloon, Hong Kong   Tel. 2376.2062
Telefax: 2376.0685

HUNGARY – HONGRIE
Euro Info Service
Margitsziget, Európa Ház
1138 Budapest   Tel. (1) 111.62.16
Telefax : (1) 111.60.61

ICELAND – ISLANDE
Mál Mog Menning
Laugavegi 18, Pósthólf 392
121 Reykjavik   Tel. 162.35.23

INDIA – INDE
Oxford Book and Stationery Co.
Scindia House
New Delhi 110001   Tel.(11) 331.5896/5308
Telefax: (11) 332.5993
17 Park Street
Calcutta 700016   Tel. 240832

INDONESIA – INDONÉSIE
Pdii-Lipi
P.O. Box 4298
Jakarta 12042   Tel. (21) 573.34.67
Telefax: (21) 573.34.67

IRELAND – IRLANDE
Government Supplies Agency
Publications Section
4/5 Harcourt Road
Dublin 2   Tel. 661.31.11
Telefax: 478.06.45

ISRAEL
Praedicta
5 Shatner Street
P.O. Box 34030
Jerusalem 91430   Tel. (2) 52.84.90/1/2
Telefax: (2) 52.84.93
R.O.Y.
P.O. Box 13056
Tel Aviv 61130   Tél. (3) 49.61.08
Telefax (3) 544.60.39

ITALY – ITALIE
Libreria Commissionaria Sansoni
Via Duca di Calabria 1/1
50125 Firenze   Tel. (055) 64.54.15
Telefax: (055) 64.12.57
Via Bartolini 29
20155 Milano   Tel. (02) 36.50.83
Editrice e Libreria Herder
Piazza Montecitorio 120
00186 Roma   Tel. 679.46.28
Telefax: 678.47.51
Libreria Hoepli
Via Hoepli 5
20121 Milano   Tel. (02) 86.54.46
Telefax: (02) 805.28.86
Libreria Scientifica
Dott. Lucio de Biasio 'Aeiou'
Via Coronelli, 6
20146 Milano   Tel. (02) 48.95.45.52
Telefax: (02) 48.95.45.48

JAPAN – JAPON
OECD Publications and Information Centre
Landic Akasaka Building
2-3-4 Akasaka, Minato-ku
Tokyo 107   Tel. (81.3) 3586.2016
Telefax: (81.3) 3584.7929

KOREA – CORÉE
Kyobo Book Centre Co. Ltd.
P.O. Box 1658, Kwang Hwa Moon
Seoul   Tel. 730.78.91
Telefax: 735.00.30

MALAYSIA – MALAISIE
University of Malaya Bookshop
University of Malaya
P.O. Box 1127, Jalan Pantai Baru
59700 Kuala Lumpur
Malaysia   Tel. 756.5000/756.5425
Telefax: 756.3246

MEXICO – MEXIQUE
Revistas y Periodicos Internacionales S.A. de C.V.
Florencia 57 - 1004
Mexico, D.F. 06600   Tel. 207.81.00
Telefax : 208.39.79

NETHERLANDS – PAYS-BAS
SDU Uitgeverij Plantijnstraat
Externe Fondsen
Postbus 20014
2500 EA's-Gravenhage   Tel. (070) 37.89.880
Voor bestellingen: Telefax: (070) 34.75.778

NEW ZEALAND
NOUVELLE-ZÉLANDE
Legislation Services
P.O. Box 12418
Thorndon, Wellington   Tel. (04) 496.5652
        Telefax: (04) 496.5698

NORWAY – NORVÈGE
Narvesen Info Center – NIC
Bertrand Narvesens vei 2
P.O. Box 6125 Etterstad
0602 Oslo 6   Tel. (022) 57.33.00
        Telefax: (022) 68.19.01

PAKISTAN
Mirza Book Agency
65 Shahrah Quaid-E-Azam
Lahore 54000   Tel. (42) 353.601
        Telefax: (42) 231.730

PHILIPPINE – PHILIPPINES
International Book Center
5th Floor, Filipinas Life Bldg.
Ayala Avenue
Metro Manila   Tel. 81.96.76
        Telex 23312 RHP PH

PORTUGAL
Livraria Portugal
Rua do Carmo 70-74
Apart. 2681
1200 Lisboa   Tel.: (01) 347.49.82/5
        Telefax: (01) 347.02.64

SINGAPORE – SINGAPOUR
Gower Asia Pacific Pte Ltd.
Golden Wheel Building
41, Kallang Pudding Road, No. 04-03
Singapore 1334   Tel. 741.5166
        Telefax: 742.9356

SPAIN – ESPAGNE
Mundi-Prensa Libros S.A.
Castelló 37, Apartado 1223
Madrid 28001   Tel. (91) 431.33.99
        Telefax: (91) 575.39.98

Libreria Internacional AEDOS
Consejo de Ciento 391
08009 – Barcelona   Tel. (93) 488.30.09
        Telefax: (93) 487.76.59

Llibreria de la Generalitat
Palau Moja
Rambla dels Estudis, 118
08002 – Barcelona
        (Subscripcions) Tel. (93) 318.80.12
        (Publicacions) Tel. (93) 302.67.23
        Telefax: (93) 412.18.54

SRI LANKA
Centre for Policy Research
c/o Colombo Agencies Ltd.
No. 300-304, Galle Road
Colombo 3   Tel. (1) 574240, 573551-2
        Telefax: (1) 575394, 510711

SWEDEN – SUÈDE
Fritzes Information Center
Box 16356
Regeringsgatan 12
106 47 Stockholm   Tel. (08) 690.90.90
        Telefax: (08) 20.50.21

Subscription Agency/Agence d'abonnements :
Wennergren-Williams Info AB
P.O. Box 1305
171 25 Solna   Tel. (08) 705.97.50
        Téléfax : (08) 27.00.71

SWITZERLAND – SUISSE
Maditec S.A. (Books and Periodicals - Livres
et périodiques)
Chemin des Palettes 4
Case postale 266
1020 Renens VD 1   Tel. (021) 635.08.65
        Telefax: (021) 635.07.80

Librairie Payot S.A.
4, place Pépinet
CP 3212
1002 Lausanne   Tel. (021) 341.33.47
        Telefax: (021) 341.33.45

Librairie Unilivres
6, rue de Candolle
1205 Genève   Tel. (022) 320.26.23
        Telefax: (022) 329.73.18

Subscription Agency/Agence d'abonnements :
Dynapresse Marketing S.A.
38 avenue Vibert
1227 Carouge   Tel.: (022) 308.07.89
        Telefax : (022) 308.07.99

See also – Voir aussi :
OECD Publications and Information Centre
August-Bebel-Allee 6
D-53175 Bonn (Germany)   Tel. (0228) 959.120
        Telefax: (0228) 959.12.17

TAIWAN – FORMOSE
Good Faith Worldwide Int'l. Co. Ltd.
9th Floor, No. 118, Sec. 2
Chung Hsiao E. Road
Taipei   Tel. (02) 391.7396/391.7397
        Telefax: (02) 394.9176

THAILAND – THAÏLANDE
Suksit Siam Co. Ltd.
113, 115 Fuang Nakhon Rd.
Opp. Wat Rajbopith
Bangkok 10200   Tel. (662) 225.9531/2
        Telefax: (662) 222.5188

TURKEY – TURQUIE
Kültür Yayinlari Is-Türk Ltd. Sti.
Atatürk Bulvari No. 191/Kat 13
Kavaklidere/Ankara   Tel. 428.11.40 Ext. 2458
Dolmabahce Cad. No. 29
Besiktas/Istanbul   Tel. 260.71.88
        Telex: 43482B

UNITED KINGDOM – ROYAUME-UNI
HMSO
Gen. enquiries   Tel. (071) 873 0011
Postal orders only:
P.O. Box 276, London SW8 5DT
Personal Callers HMSO Bookshop
49 High Holborn, London WC1V 6HB
        Telefax: (071) 873 8200
Branches at: Belfast, Birmingham, Bristol, Edin-
burgh, Manchester

UNITED STATES – ÉTATS-UNIS
OECD Publications and Information Centre
2001 L Street N.W., Suite 700
Washington, D.C. 20036-4910 Tel. (202) 785.6323
        Telefax: (202) 785.0350

VENEZUELA
Libreria del Este
Avda F. Miranda 52, Aptdo. 60337
Edificio Galipán
Caracas 106   Tel. 951.1705/951.2307/951.1297
        Telegram: Libreste Caracas

Subscription to OECD periodicals may also be
placed through main subscription agencies.

Les abonnements aux publications périodiques de
l'OCDE peuvent être souscrits auprès des
principales agences d'abonnement.

Orders and inquiries from countries where Distribu-
tors have not yet been appointed should be sent to:
OECD Publications Service, 2 rue André-Pascal,
75775 Paris Cedex 16, France.

Les commandes provenant de pays où l'OCDE n'a
pas encore désigné de distributeur peuvent être
adressées à : OCDE, Service des Publications,
2, rue André-Pascal, 75775 Paris Cedex 16, France.

1-1995

PRINTED IN FRANCE

•

OECD PUBLICATIONS
2, rue André-Pascal
75775 PARIS CEDEX 16
No. 47901
(10 95 04 1) ISBN 92-64-14461-7
ISSN 0376-6438

•

OECD
ECONOMIC
SURVEYS

Latest Surveys Available:

AUSTRALIA, MAY 1995

AUSTRIA, MAY 1995

BELGIUM-LUXEMBOURG, JANUARY 1994

CANADA, NOVEMBER 1994

DENMARK, AUGUST 1994

FINLAND, FEBRUARY 1995

FRANCE, MARCH 1994

GERMANY, AUGUST 1994

GREECE, MARCH 1995

ICELAND, MAY 1995

IRELAND, JUNE 1993

ITALY, JANUARY 1995

JAPAN, NOVEMBER 1994

MEXICO, SEPTEMBER 1992

NETHERLANDS, AUGUST 1994

NEW ZEALAND, OCTOBER 1994

NORWAY, MARCH 1994

PORTUGAL, JUNE 1994

SPAIN, JUNE 1994

SWEDEN, JANUARY 1994

SWITZERLAND, AUGUST 1994

TURKEY, APRIL 1995

UNITED KINGDOM, JULY 1994

UNITED STATES, NOVEMBER 1994

Surveys of "Partners in Transition" Countries

HUNGARY, SEPTEMBER 1993

THE CZECH AND SLOVAK REPUBLICS, FEBRUARY 1994

POLAND, JANUARY 1995

Non-member Country

KOREA, MAY 1994

(10 95 04 1)   UXX
ISBN 92-64-14461-7
ISSN 0376-6438

1995 Subscription
France: FF 1 200
All other countries: FF 1 300 US$240 DM 398

OECD

ECONOMIC

SURVEYS

NORWAY

1995